From Dog Collar to Dog Collar

From Dog Collar to Dog Collar

Bruce Howat

From Dog Collar to Dog Collar
Published by Rangitawa Publishing, Feilding, New Zealand.

ISBN 978-0-9951406-0-8

www.rangitawapublishing.com
rangitawa@xtra,co,nz

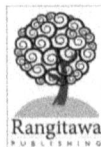

Rangitawa
PUBLISHING

Reviews

From Dog Collar to Dog Collar.

Bruce through narrative invites us into his life in two distinct paths that he has walked. These paths have the common thread of the 'dog collar' as he shares his life as a policeman and a Christian minister. This journey over many years has had a number of twists and turns that have dramatically changed the course of Bruce's life and as we walk this path with him through these stories we can see that life does not always pan out as we might imagine. Decisions are made, often due to circumstances beyond our control. Sometimes we catch a glimpse of the One who may be leading and directing that path whether our service is in the church or in the community. Both vocations have immense value to society affecting other people's lives and those lives are often encountered during moments of extreme suffering or difficulty. Bruce offers to us a touch of compassion that puts people first in his eyes. This compassion is seen for both victims and perpetrators as he exposes his love for humanity. Bruce's story raises that thought and opens up the idea that through triumphs and trials life has meaning and purpose. Thank you Bruce for taking us on this journey with you.

Richard Gray – Friend and colleague

I have had the privilege of reading Bruce Howat's new book "From dog collar to dog collar" after he asked me to do a review. Bruce and I have a common past, both ex police and both ex-dog handlers. We also worked together briefly in Lower Hutt on section duties in the 1970s and I have always considered him a good mate and a cracker cop.

Bruce's book was a march back in time for me, his detailed use of imagery brought back all the sights, smells and sounds of policing, particularly policing at night time on one's own. His description of heightened senses when in danger or approaching a dangerous situation is vivid and very real. Street cops like Bruce was live on their nerves knowing that violence is very near and very real and, as younger people, knowing that they may not see loved ones again unless they are very careful or very quick.

Bruce was what is described as a General Dog Handler. As such he was also an aide to his local Armed Offenders Section. These dog handlers' lives are dangerous to the extreme. They are the first into houses after their dogs, first in line on a track, the first cop an offender sees and often attacks or shoots at. Personal serious injury is common. Bruce's description of the stabbing injuries that led him to leave the police is harrowing and very personal. The cost to Bruce of this injury, losing his career, his marriage and his ready access to his beloved daughters is personally tragic and not unusually sad in modern policing. When this is coupled with the thoughtless treatment meted out by the police in removing his new dog, indicating that he was being written off as a dog handler, one can understand the damage this did to Bruce's recovery.

Bruce describes his new life post-police as a university student, finding happiness again when meeting the love of his life Suraya, herself now a successful author, and subsequently qualifying as a Presbyterian Minister whilst also acquiring a very respectable number of high academic qualifications along the way. He tal of the street he inhabited as a young man trying to serve and protect his community. Submerged into parish life he also talks about falling back on his past skills as a cop to help parishioners and their families in times of joy, stress and loss.

Bruce and I share a liberal view of the world and of politics; some would say we are lefties, unusual in the eyes of some bearing in mind our background as front-line police. Bruce talked of his vocation for the church as a teenager prior to his joining the police. He is not unlike others who enter the religious ministry after many years of policing; the vocational calling was always there in the background.

Post-Traumatic Stress Syndrome arising from his stabbing became a crippling disorder for Bruce. He describes in detail how he faced his demons later in life and learned how to come to grips with them and to live with them.

His is a very human story of compassion and pragmatism coupled with his love of his God and I recommend it to readers as a story of one man who has been to hell and back, coming out the other side as a complete and very accomplished individual.

Robert Rattenbury (ex Armed Offenders Squad)

Dedicated to

*My grandparents who had the courage to leave their ancestral grounds,
to search for a better place for the next generations
My parents who taught and were love
My great and grandchildren – welcome to part of Granddad's world
To my children who brought me back
My beautiful wife, Suraya, who believed in me when I did not
Thank you all for your part in shaping me*

*I also acknowledge the inspirational, courageous members of the Police I
had the privilege to work alongside. You are unsung heroes of our
community.
To my Minister colleagues, continue in the faith, having the courage to
often physically stand alone, having faith in something bigger than us.
Continue in servanthood.
Words cannot express my full thanks to Flo Ginsburg, Los Angeles,
not only for her wonderful editing skills, but also words of
encouragement. Your attention to detail is fantastic!*

Why?

The natural order of things is a parent dies before their children, but it still does not feel right. Parents are supposed to be forever. Riddled with cancer; I gave up counting Dad's various types. He was an unemotional man, a product of his Scottish upbringing. A devout Christian Minister, it always felt the people in his Parishes got more of his feelings than I did as a kid. Yet I loved him and knew missing him was my future reality.

Dad asked me to play a dual role in his last phase of life – continue being his son, but also his Minister. I am an ordained Presbyterian Minister and yet religion is something we could not discuss – our views very different. Dad, being Dad, was super organised and wrote his own funeral. As his Minister, I needed to respect the confidentiality of what he shared, until his service.

Dad's funeral was the toughest and easiest, ever – toughest emotionally and easiest because he had written his story. Everyone learns something new at a good funeral and I met my father for the first time through his service.

Reflecting later on, I realised my grandkids knew nothing about me, and so I started writing my memoirs of part of my life. I am not a literary writer; my style is me wanting to "chat" with you.

This collection of personal stories is divided into two distinct parts:
1. Police dog collar
2. Minister's dog collar

Some will connect with aspects of my Police career and struggle with the Minister part. Others, the other way around. But collectively, they give an insight into what makes me tick, well as close as I am prepared to share and also (I hope) show that none of us actually fit in nice boxes, we are complex creatures trying to find our unique spot in a strange world.

To the reader

We all have stories to tell – our future generations are shaped by us, and yet, do they know the real us as seen by ourselves. Have the courage to tell your own story.

Chapters

The journey into my first dog collar

Police Training College 1972

Why I wanted to join the Police was a well-hidden mystery. At a logical level I have no idea why I wanted it, all I know, something internal directed me into this career option.

Acceptance into the Police became a two-year battle. It started with me walking into the old Waihi Police Station during my lunch break as a bank teller. Sergeant Bowerman was reading a Police manual, with his bum strategically placed against the open fire, so he gets all the warmth, and none escapes into the room. Sergeant Bowerman was a huge 6′5 Fijian and he has won the community with his powerful laugh, but also his no-nonsense approach.

I asked him "what are the chances of getting into the Police with glasses." He hardly looked up and announced "none!" I turned to leave the room.

"We wouldn't have you anyway!"

"If that's the fight you have in you, lad, you won't last two seconds on the street."

I saw red, spun around, and challenged him.
And so, began my two-year battle to prove I was the right stuff to be a good street cop. The only reason they kept rejecting me was my eyesight – evidently, I flew through all the other tests. Then election year arrived, and the government of the day was using law & order as one of their driving policies. The decision to put through the largest wing of trainee tested the recruiters to the extreme. Those (like me) who had been rejected on one ground, they reconsidered. our cases. My eyesight was not as bad as they first thought.

On Friday 3rd September 1972, I went to the Hamilton Central Police Station to swear in officially with seven other budding trainees. We received rail passes for the overnight train to Wellington for the Monday morning start. I went home that night with the full arrest powers of a New Zealand Police Constable and no idea what it meant.

On the Saturday, at the family Bach at Waihi Beach we celebrated my 20th birthday. In those days, the custom was to have 21st birthday parties as the coming of age rituals, but we had no idea where I was going to be stationed and what the future held.

I was the youngest of my Police counter parts; Dick had been in the Met Police in London and had been recruited to come to New Zealand. He took a shine to me and we chatted for hours on the overnight train. The train, scientifically designed to save the careers of trained chiropractors, rearranged my spine every few miles.

At seven a.m. we arrived at Wellington Central Railway Station – peak rush hour for the city commuters. The innocent country boy was starting his education. Looking out the window, I watched two males in pin stripe suits giving each other a passionate goodbye kiss. My disbelieving eyes were in shock, horror, and bewilderment. Dick hit me on the arm and bought me out of my trance. I grabbed my bag with all my worldly possessions and disembarking the train, saw nearby the old bus with Police emblem. Then the roar of a voice through a megaphone:

"All Police recruits over here and form three lines, at the double." This voice haunted me for the next three months. Senior Sergeant Tom Bidois (RIP). My military style Police training had begun.

The bus drove us to Wellington South to the uniform store to get our black serge Police uniforms. I walked in procession with all the others and learnt to keep my mouth quiet. The store staff just threw items of uniform at us to put into our kit bags. A guy ahead of me in the line protested that what he was given would not fit him – it was too small. Nothing was said. He was then given another item two size's smaller with a "next." Back on the bus, we bartered amongst ourselves until we got uniforms that semi-fitted.

Then the bus trip out to Trentham. The college housed in old army barracks – where insulation and warmth were not basic requirements.

Trentham involved nearly every day in a classroom, but it started with a parade first thing, with uniform inspection. We then marched to "Luigi's" - the mess hall where the attempt at getting rid of us through food poisoning seemed to be the aim. After "breakfast" it was back to our rooms for barrack inspection. Anything found wrong meant a run around the water tower the next morning before the daily ritual started. The water tower was situated on a pine tree clad hill, watching over the camp. My roommate and I were determined we would go through the three months training and not be sent around the tower.

It was a bit of a silly target at one level, I was running around the tower every morning, just to try and keep some level of fitness. I'd been labouring before being accepted (I left the bank because I thought I had better get to know my future clients). Sitting all day in a classroom and studying Police manuals and laws was all very well and good, but my fitness was suffering.

When we started at the College, we all had to do a regulation fitness level test, knowing there would be another at the end. The "fitness training" was to get us ready for work on the streets and we were constantly assured we would leave the college fitter than when we arrived. I was one of two who lost fitness levels during the course – the other guy came from a farm.

Every Saturday morning, we sat a three-hour exam on the law we had learnt that week. We had to know the law verbatim, even getting commas and full stops in the right place. The pass mark was sixty five percent. I was a school dropout, with minus academic confidence, but riddled with stubbornness and determination. I was going to graduate as a cop, if it killed me. I did fail one exam, not by much but still a fail. The reward. The following week I had two three-hour exams to sit. I had to redo the fail one to a pass level as well as pass the current week's one. I was up all hours of every night trying to learn this stuff.

Graduation eventually came. My parents came down for the event, and so did my then girlfriend – we had been going together for a while before I went to Trentham. I was easy to find in the graduation parade. Those of us with two left feet were strategically placed inside our unit so that hopefully, no one could notice that I couldn't march in time. The Police Pipe Band played and us marching retards were told to make sure that when the bass drum was hit, left feet were placed on the ground. I almost fell twice, so busy trying to make sure I heard the blasted drum, I got myself confused as to which foot should be hitting the deck.

It made no difference to Mum & Dad; they were glowing with pride. It felt a bit ironical because Dad threatened to ban me from the family, because he never wanted me to join – he wanted me to follow in his footsteps. My girlfriend was also proud, and to this day I believe she was genuine in what she said.

After the parade we found out where we were all posted. It was a great process only Police hierarchy could come up with. We were to apply for three stations, in order of preference with reasons for wishing to be posted there. I was going to Wellington Central. The closest place to Wellington I had applied for was Tauranga. It felt a bit like a solid kidney punch. I broke the news to the family – it was very mixed reactions from them. Mum did not see how I would cope, being so far away from the family. My girlfriend was silent.

That night we had the graduation ball, a grand affair. The next day my girlfriend, who was from Hamilton, broke up with me. She could not see how we could have a meaningful relationship when we were going to be so far apart, and I was focusing on learning to be a good cop. There was no animosity and never has been.

2

The beating on the beat

It was hard in that split second to decide whether the tyres were radial or standard tread; they just looked black, fast and ominous.

My night on the beat was normal, lots of walking, very slowly, just watching. Walking the beat taught patience, perseverance but most importantly, it taught observation skills. We had two kinds of beat duties; block beat meant you had a section of the city to patrol as you saw fit. Section beat meant all on the beat walked the same route but were 15 minutes apart. Block beat was only for the night shift and there was a sense of pride no crime happened in your "block" during the shift.

I started every shift with my spit and polished shoes, my uniform ironed so you could cut your fingers on the crease. Training school days instilled the discipline of appearance. I didn't know why I always got the same block as it had all the strip clubs and a number of inner-city bars. The clubs were places where many crimes hatched and dispatched.

I was walking along Manners Street, Wellington Central,

heading towards Taranaki Street. It was just after 11p.m. and there was a hotel down a side street. I regularly stood on the corner and let my uniform do the talking. The drunks staggering out of the hotel at closing time were at their poetic best as they described my presence. William Shakespeare would have been proud of the English language used by drunks leaving the hotel. The lesson I learnt was to be silent and let the abuse careen off my uniform. The logic in my head was the abuse was at my uniform and what it stood for rather than me as a person.

This night the crowd radiated a different energy. Usually there was lots of laughter and good-hearted fun, but this night had a rough edge. The feeling from a mob varied and often it was hard to pinpoint exactly what made it feel different, but tonight did. Our beat radios were useless in 1972. On my beat they only worked in a couple of spots, luckily this was one. I radioed in trouble was brewing without any concrete evidence. It was an inner instinct – gut feeling never stacking up in a law Court.

How the fight started and who started it I don't know. The surprise for me it broke out only a few feet away. Suddenly knucklebones collided with jaws bones with the clank of wood on wood sound effect. The Police uniform was black serge and very baggy trousers, which was a blessing in disguise, no one ever saw how often my knees knocked. No one had any idea; on the inside I was nervous and scared. The human body was a fascinating machine, from relaxed docile into adrenaline fear and anxiety within fractions of a second. The fear was a crowd of a couple of hundred and a sole Policeman, me. This was my first time of a crowd going feral for no apparent reason and my uniform, instead of protecting me was the target.

I never said a word when the first punch hit me in the side of the head, knocking my helmet off. Blows were hitting me everywhere across my chest and face. I remembered the advice of a senior constable; "never go down, they will kill you if you hit the deck." My adrenaline was on overdrive and I feared for my own safety. Thank goodness, I had radioed in before the scene escalated. A patrol car cruised around the corner from Willis Street into Manners Street. By this stage, the street closed with a brawling mob. The urgency of the situation must have registered with the guys in the patrol car.

I cannot remember how many of them picked me up, but suddenly I found myself flying over the bonnet of a parked car and no superman cape to help. I hit the road with a painstaking thud. I was looking towards Willis Street, face and body on the road. It was hard in a split second to decide whether the tyres were radial or standard tread; they just looked black, fast and ominous. I managed to roll my head clear and felt the car tyres pull a few pieces of hair from my head. Fear was my closest ally; the next car was the patrol car. Two colleagues jumped out with batons drawn and stood guard over me lying on the ground. The crowd saw the new form of entertainment and came to deal to the three of us. I got to my feet as quickly as I could and drew my baton.

In those days NZ Police did not have sirens, only flashing lights so we had no idea how far away help was. The survival saying, "fight or flight" was in my head. There was no escape, so flight removed itself from the equation. Now there were three of us against a few hundred; much better odds. In the situation one second felt like an hour, everything around me moved in slow motion. The rulebook went out the door; we had no interest in the protocol for using our batons – our lives were on the line. Adrenalin prevented me feeling any pain.

This was scary at its finest.

Down at the Taranaki Street intersection we saw more flashing lights arrive; in the fight, I was checking every direction at once. Outnumbered was not a great feeling. Then around the corner from Willis Street came the large grey prison van with its little red-light flashing. The cavalry arriving bought a sense of relief and hope. It just drove into the crowd until the back door was beside us. The Sergeant driving yelled at us to get in the back and for once, I was more than happy to obey an order. We had to baton away the street Vikings. They just kept coming at us until we were able to close the door. Then the van drove through the crowd to the other Police vehicles.

My colleagues called an Ambulance. I resisted going away from the action, but more experienced voices convinced me I needed to see a Doctor. While waiting I watched the back of the prison van filled up with excited customers anticipating a free night on the government.

An enquiry took place after the event, but no one could identify what triggered an explosive night.

All I had was severe bruising, but I was judged to be fit for another night's work, even though uncomfortable and in considerable pain. This was the first of three trips to Hospital in my first twelve months as a street Policeman. There was a long gap before the fourth trip arrived, maybe I was a slow learner.

Most of my colleagues thought walking the beat was boring but I got more than my fair share of action on the streets.

3

The night ghosts

My secret goal on night shift beat, was to catch a burglar o the job, my wits against his. I enjoyed crawling across the rooftops, hidden from the sight of those on the streets. Our heavy serge trousers had a long pocket on the left side for a torch, and one on the right for our short, stubby wooden baton. I rarely pulled either one out. If I wanted to catch a burglar, I didn't want to give away my location.

I was walking across the dimly lit station yard, when Sergeant Clint called out. "wait up Bruce, I will drop you off on your beat!" I was happy to walk, but he insisted. So, I shuffled around in the yard, wanting to get onto the street. Eventually he arrived and I jumped into his patrol car.

As we were driving through Lambton Quay, he told me that the Police Mortuary was insecure. A Funeral Director had backed into the external door and wrecked the lock. A locksmith wasn't available until tomorrow. I was to spend the night in the mortuary as a guard. I respected the need for a guard, but equally was disappointed I could not look after my patch.

I was able to help myself to coffee, and Clint would drop me off a meal during the night. I was not allowed to turn on any lights, as the Mortuary was in the middle of my beat area and very few of the public knew what the building was for.

I never complained and was not nervous, there was nothing to be nervous about. At this point in my life I had seen two dead bodies. Dead was dead was my logic. So, I went into the Mortuary for an exciting night – not! Mortuaries have their own unique smell, a mixture of powerful disinfectant combined with the unique smell of death. They also had silence, lots of silence. The silence did not worry me, as I am a strong introvert and preferred it to noise.

I went into the waiting room, after my initial wander through, checking everything. There were a couple of bodies in there, lying on their trolley with a white sheet over them, just the bare feet sticking out with the standard luggage label tied to the big toe with a piece of brown string. The waiting room had a couple of comfortable, brown leather chairs, showing their age and use, but good resting places. In there I knew it was about the only place my portable radio would work. The silence meant if anyone tried to get in, the external doors make so much noise when opening, I could not miss that noise.

One of the differences of a mortuary waiting room compared to a Doctor or Dentist one, was they have no terrible intelligence insulting magazines to flick through. Just a couple of chairs with a small plain metal coffee table in between. The kitchen was close, and had a skylight, so it was the only room with some form of lighting, albeit very little. My biggest worry was falling asleep, mainly because it would put me out of my night shift sleep patterns.

So, the night settled into my pattern of waiting for about fifty minutes of every hour, and then a wander through the facilities. I always offered to two laid out residents a cup of coffee, but they were laid back and never responded, in fact I found their attitude a bit stiff.

About halfway through the night Sergeant Clint arrived with my dinner, stating he could not stay long as they were flat out. My radio meant I only had access to those others on the beat and the Operations room. It was not uncommon for there to be no talk all night. The patrol cars might be flat out and those on the beat had no idea it was a busy shift.

My one piece of stimulation, eating the meal on my own did not last long. My company was my mind, which was entertaining itself with hearing non-existent noises. For example, I thought our two bodies were having a chat, maybe they were but when I went to check, they just lay there, stiff as boards. Then the mind would go on a fascinating exercise, wondering what two dead people, who hadn't known each other before, what would they talk about.

Time dragged and my two-house guests were extremely boring. I did learn the concept of scent assimilation, because it hadn't taken long for the smell of the mortuary to become my new normality.

What did change over time was my jumpiness. Any imagined sound got me jumpy, which defies logic, but it did happen. The bleached tiled walls started to develop patterns to entertain me. Eight hours in this environment made for the most unusual night, and it was a major sigh of relief when a day shift replacement arrived. I was proud how I survived a night with the dead.

4

Chris goes down

Chris was different to most of my other Police colleagues. He was minimum height, wavy blonde hair, blues eyes and athletic build. It was not his physical appearance that separated him from the others, but he was the only fellow Policeman I worked with who was not only a Ballroom Dancer but has won numerous awards for his efforts. I think it was because he was different, I enjoyed working with him.

The Police in the early 1970's were macho. History can look unkindly at the behaviours, but we had next to no equipment and very little radio communication. We carried our notebooks, a plastic torch on night shift and a small wooden baton. The batons were very useful at minor motor accidents for prising mudguards off wheels and saving the cost of a tow truck.

Chris and I were on patrol in Lower Hutt. At Stokes Valley shops, we did a foot patrol. We take pride in making the business community feel safe. We wandered around the shops, checking that all doors and windows are secure. Burglar alarms are not very prolific.

We parked the patrol car in the car park and radioed in that we were going to be out of contact for fifteen minutes while we check the shops. Even at this early stage in my career, I am not renowned for carrying my torch. My dream was to catch a burglar on the job through my own initiative and a torch meant potential burglars see me coming.

It was a cold; windy winter's night and we are wearing Police Regulation Great Coats.

Chris and I have been on patrol together all week, and so when Sunday night came, we made an unusual decision for us. We would walk together. Normally we split up to save time and do a thorough job. One would head one way around the shops while the other did the opposite direction.

Stokes Valley was a state housing estate., all government-built houses that all look the same and have the same interior design. The government picks the colours etc. An era not exposed to individuality. One thing these settlements do create was a sense of community. Therefore, when Chris and I walked around the back of the shops and found a group of young teenagers we were not surprised.

Chris was very amiable, friendly and loves talking to young people and so he walks up to them to start a conversation. There are about 15-20 young people and the oldest may be fifteen. They are doing nothing to raise any alarm bells, just a bunch of teenagers out late at night. Chris has only started to say hello when without warning the first young fellow throws a punch at him. It was laughable; the kid was lucky if he was twelve. Chris does not believe what happened and asks the kid "what was that all about." Another punch and then another kid start punching Chris, time for intervention.

I move in "to sort these kids out" when I am punched in the back. I turn around and there was another group of kids. This group came out of the darkness. Suddenly Chris and I realised we were the entertainment of the night. We were in the middle of about thirty plus, bored, frustrated young people and our only radio contact, via our patrol car about seventy yards away.

Then the feeding frenzy begins, youths climbing over us with fists and boots flaying. Our larger size was irrelevant because we are so outnumbered. The only good aspect was they are hitting our bodies, encased in the large great coats. I suspected they watched Dad knock Mum around and knew not to hit the face for fear of leaving obvious wounds. Chris and I are about twenty feet apart, Chris being the furthest from the patrol car.

"Call for help," he bellowed.

Calling for help was not easy as I have about twelve to fifteen youths converting me into a jungle gym for them to climb over. I make a conscious decision not to get my baton out for fear of them getting it off me. I know the request from Chris was the correct thing to do, and so swatting flies trying to land on me I slowly make progress to the patrol car. I am unclear how long it takes to get there.

I heard the Operations room asking another patrol to head towards Stokes Valley because we have been off the air for too long.

I realised as I get close to the patrol car that there was a high risk of these kids getting the patrol car keys off me. Then I heard the Upper Hutt Patrol say they are nearby and will check us out.

I was pinned against the patrol car trying to work out how to get the car open and call for help. I looked across the car park, I cannot see Chris, just a crowd of young people looking down and jumping around. They must have Chris on the ground.

As quickly as I threw one away another two punches. Chris being on the ground was serious and caution goes. I reached into my pocket for the car keys and one of the kids decided I am trying to get my baton out. This causes a bigger frenzy. I forgot about the keys and the ages of the offenders. My fists start flying at faces and anything in the path of my knuckles.

My peripheral vision caught something. A red flashing light. The Upper Hutt car has arrived. Luckily, they were at the Trentham Police College when they decided to check us out. They have one of the instructors and a recruit with them. The four of them came to my rescue. They radioed in what was happening prior to stopping.

I yelled at the Sergeant that Chris was in the middle of the other mob. The extra numbers are not a deterrent to the kids, almost the opposite. The instructor and recruit stayed with me while the two Upper Hutt staff tried to get to Chris. This was civil warfare. Instead of two fighting for their lives, now there are six of us in the same predicament. Most fights last a few minutes because everyone runs out of steam. Someone forgot to tell these young people.

Then two more cars arrived from Lower Hutt. The situation was slowly starting to get under control except for the fact that other kids were arriving from neighbouring houses. Then the Lower Hutt Sergeant arrived with the big prison van and yells, "let's fill it up." After throwing the first few in the back, the newcomers decided to back off.

Without warning three patrol cars from Wellington Central arrived. Now we have numbers to get the situation under control. Through this whole process, I had been unable to sight Chris.

"Get an Ambulance here fast," yelled one of the Upper Hutt crew.

The Prison van was able to accommodate about twenty youths who were going to get to taste the Hospitality of Her Majesty's cells for a night. The Ambulance rushed Chris to Hospital.

****

Chris physically recovered, but the emotional scars of that night never left him. I was lucky I managed to keep to my feet. I suffered bruising, but if neither of us were wearing great coats, it was too scary to think what our injuries might have been.

5

An unforgettable death

The first dead body I ever saw was my maternal grandmother. I had been very close to her and her death, even though from old age, hurt.

I was on night shift in Lower Hutt and it was an average night for crime. Then the call most of us dread came over the radio at 1:30a.m.

"Sudden death XX Avenue Stokes Valley." There was never anything pleasant about them and all you could hope for was a clean body. The rotten ones were – well… rotten.

My partner and I had all the required forms with us in the patrol car and headed to the address. This was not a lights flashing job, in fact, we drove with the sombreness of a laden hearse. Conversation was almost non-existent. As we got near the address, we split up the work. The choice was easy; one to deal with the family, the other with the body and mortuary duty. At the address there was crossover, both helping each other out, but once the body left we then went into our separate roles. I was to deal with the family.

The hardest thing about attending a sudden death was no crime had been committed and yet the family had the humiliation of the Police taking away their loved one. The reality was a requirement under the Coroner's Act, that if a registered medical practitioner couldn't certify cause of death, it requires an investigation by the Coroner and the Police (by law) are the Coroner's Agents.

We had no information as to what we were attending except Ambulance had requested us. Our hope was to get a Doctor to certify cause and we could get out of there. My partner and I assembled the correct paperwork in our folders and braced ourselves for what was ahead. One of the Ambulance Officers met us at the front step.

"Thirty-two-year-old female dead. She has been suffering severe stomach pains all night and by the time we got here, she was gone. The husband was distraught, and they have a three year old who was asleep at the moment and unaware of what has happened."

Great, a horrible emotional one!

We both walked in with our patrol caps off. It was one of the few times the bosses would not rollick us for failing to wear our caps. The husband was slumped over the dining room table. My guess was he would be a couple of years older than his wife, but tonight he had the weight of the world on his shoulders.

We both stumbled out an apology for being in his home at this time under these circumstances. I had only just turned twenty-one, with very little life experience and here I am expected to comfort and console this poor guy. We explained why we are there and where could we find his wife. The house was very plain, no carpets, just wooden floors. He points down the hall and we see bedroom doors off both sides. All these state houses looked the same inside and out. We knew through experience which room was supposed to be the master bedroom. My partner and I were overly self-conscious of the noise of our Police regulation shoes on the wooden floor.

I went in the room first. On the bed was the naked body. It was obvious she had died an incredibly painful death. The problem was we had to treat it as a suspicious death until we had evidence to the contrary. We took half the room each to check if there was anything suspicious – there was not. Then we had to do a body examination, again for anything suspicious. All the time the dead body watched us invade her privacy. The body still had beads of perspiration, another clue this death was not a pleasant one.

Now our duties split. I had to talk to the husband to establish what went on. The "talk" had to be a mixture of sympathy and suspicion. I was single with no children – how do you fake empathy? How do you hide suspicion? Technically there are no grounds to be suspicious, but the training makes it that you never let your guard down for fear of missing something.

The husband told me his wife, while preparing tea in their little kitchen, started to get stomach cramps. As the evening wore on, she was in more and more pain. His concern was growing so he rang the family GP to be told to ring in the morning and make an appointment at the clinic. The GP had asked virtually no questions and the husband left the call feeling chastised. Four more times during the night he rang the GP as his wife deteriorated. On the last call, the GP said, "If you are so bloody concerned ring a damn Ambulance."

One last question. "Why was your wife naked?"

"She was sweating so much she had gone through three nighties – there are no more, and she didn't like having to try and get the clothes on."

I was obliged to check there were three nighties in the wash basket. There were.

My partner had called a Police Doctor and had a Death Certificate, but not cause. The Funeral Director arrived, and they had taken the stretcher into the bedroom. My partner asked me to give them a hand. I went into the bedroom and we put the wife's body into a body bag on the stretcher. The Funeral Director was about to zip the bag closed when a little voice peeped through the silence, "What are you doing to Mummy?"

I was the closest to the little guy and I had no idea what to do or say. I sat down on the floor, pulled him onto my lap, and attempted to tell him Mummy had died and that we had to take her away so we could find out why. A noise at the door caught my attention. It was the husband. I have no idea how long he had been there, and silent tears rushed across the rapids of his face. Our tear floodgates were internal, as we could not afford to show how this was affecting us all.

The father took his son down to the dining room while Mummy was carried outside into the darkness of the waiting hearse. I put my arm around the father while he watched in silence. My partner went in the hearse.

I asked him who he wanted to be with him for the rest of the night. He gave me the name of his Minister and I made the call. I stayed until the Minister arrived.

"Was Mummy going to heaven?" Thank goodness the Minister was there as that was no question for a single 21-year old, naïve copper to answer. I said that I would leave them alone and went out to the Patrol car. I just sat in it for what seemed like eternity before I had the energy to fire the engine into life. I did not have a key to my own engine.

Police deal with many deaths and I had my fair share. Some the bodies were rotten, others mangled messes, but it was the emotion of the scene that affected me more than the sights and smells.

****

I complained to the Coroner about the standard of medical care. Or should I say lack of care shown to this woman. She had died of tubular pregnancy and if taken to Hospital earlier she probably would have lived. Nothing happened to the professionals and I never saw or heard from the father or son again, but I have never forgotten them or that night. Darkness took on a new meaning to me that night.

6

Everyone needs a break

Everyone needs a break from their job and Police are no different. Sole charge stations are hard for staff to get breaks, as they have to negotiate well in advance so city Police can cover.

I went to Ngatea on the Hauraki Plains; a sleepy little rural town, whose main income was from farming. I stayed at the local hotel. The Police Station attached to the Police house gave me full access to Bob, the local Policeman. Bob took the duck-shooting season off every year, so the bosses knew well in advance when he needed his breaks.

One-night Bob invited the local traffic cop and me to his house for tea. We had just settled down to a convivial evening when the phone rang. There was a serious accident on one of the main state highways.

As I was rushing out the door, Bob called out.

"It'll be a fatal; they always are in that spot."

City policing was about teamwork and back up. At Ngatea I was on my own. I rushed out to the scene about ten minute's fast drive from the Police Station. The Traffic cop followed at a distance. As I came onto the long straight, I could see the lights of parked vehicles ahead. One of the vehicles was lit up as a Christmas tree. I pulled the patrol car to the side of the road and left the red flashing lights on. The Traffic cop stopped further down the road for traffic control.

There was a milk truck on the side of the road; this was the vehicle with a large number of lights. On the road a fully laden logging truck and a car sheared in half. The milkman told me there was a man in the car in bad shape and his wife was in the farmhouse adjacent to the accident scene. It was instantly obvious the logging truck had collided with the car and first impressions were the logging truck had hit the car on the wrong side of the road.

I had to crawl up into the car to check on him. He was semi-alive. Lying alongside of him, I checked his pulse; it was very weak. He was barely able to make a sound.

The Ambulance had to came from Thames and was call out volunteers. This night was the fastest I got an Ambulance to any incident – 45 minutes. I made the decision to stay with the dying man until the Ambulance arrived. I kept looking into the darkness praying for a speedy arrival. Lying inside a wrecked car with a dying man the world feels slow motion. I kept talking to him about how help was on the way. The road was incredibly dark and there did not appear to be a moon. I will never know what was going through the driver's mind, but I was not going to let someone die alone.

After an eternity, a flashing light appeared at the end of the straight. Finally! My jubilation at the sight of the flashing lights took my concentration away from the driver. When I looked at him again, it was too late; he was dead. I slowly crawled my way out of the car and stood beside it, numb. The Ambulance crew rushed to my side – they saw my uniform covered in blood and thought I was injured. I explained that I was okay but we had a fatality in the car. I then remembered the wife inside the farmhouse. I had no idea about her injuries.

The two Ambulance officers and I rushed into the house. The wife was sitting at the kitchen table finishing another cup of tea.

She did not have a mark on her body.

This was the hardest one to break the news that her husband was dead. She could not comprehend that she was uninjured, and her husband was dead. We took her out to the car to show that he was indeed dead. She wanted to stay and watch us remove him from the wreck, which we did not initially object to. However, when we started to try to extricate the body from the car, we realised the extent of his massive injuries. His legs were coming out, but not the torso. One of the Ambulance officers took the wife back into the farmhouse.

After much discussion I crawled back into the car and tied the deceased to myself and slowly we came out together to keep the body intact. I have no recollection of the time it took, but time was not a relevant thought – dignity was more important.

The Ambulance took the body to the Thames Mortuary and I radioed the Thames Police and asked them to do that part of the accident for me. I still had a logging truck driver to deal with.

As I got near the logging truck, the driver climbed out of the cab. I could smell the alcohol on him. He was honest stating that he had stopped at the Tapu Tavern and had a few beers. I gave him a breathalyser test, which he failed. I had to take him to the Thames Police Station for further tests, but I still had a scene to clear up. The Traffic cop was still a distance down the road with his lights flashing.

Then the milk truck driver approached me. He was a former Traffic cop, he offered to organise the tow truck for me, and he would stay guard on the logging truck until I decided what to do.

I took the logging truck driver to Thames, but he was okay with the second test. He had not drunk for nearly two hours at this stage, so there was nothing more to be done in that regard. I drove him back to his truck and said we would be talking again.

I went back to the hotel where I was staying and collapsed on my bed with exhaustion. The paperwork could wait.

The next day I had to go and interview the farmers and all the other witnesses including the milk truck driver. The paperwork war was about to begin. It was early evening and I was still at the station doing the paperwork when the hotel rang.

"There's been a fight and we need an Ambulance. They are still fighting in the car park."

I rang for an Ambulance before heading down to the hotel. As I drove in, there were four males who had another pinned against a parked car and they were discussing the meaning of life as only rural folk can. I jumped in between them, as I feared for the male pinned against the car. I did not want a homicide on my hands.

"He tried to kill our mate."

"That does not justify you killing him."

I handcuffed the "victim" and put him in the back seat of the patrol car.

I approached one of the locals. "You are my deputy – guard him with your life. One more injury and I will have bits of your anatomy you will not want me possessing."

I went back into the hotel to try to make sense of the call for an Ambulance. A crowd gathered around another bloke who was bleeding profusely from his head. I went to examine him and saw a massive gash across his forehead, millimetres from his eye.

The "victim" in my car had come in and ordered a beer. He drank it and then without warning threw the glass across the bar where it smashed into a patron's face. No one knew my "victim"; he was not a local. I asked Jock the Hotelier to record all witnesses' details for me, as I had to take my prisoner to Thames. I could interview everyone later. Staying at the hotel was an advantage as Jock and I got on really well. The new victim was bandaged up enough to keep him in one piece until the Ambulance arrived about an hour later.

My "deputy" stayed in the back seat with the prisoner. I started the drive to Thames.

"You have to be the dumbest bugger I've ever known. Smashing a local in the face like that – you are lucky I was there as quick as I was, or it would be all over for you."

The answer flattened me.

I did my arrest file at Thames as I still had a fatal accident file ahead of me when I got back to Ngatea. In the file, I put the explanation given to me.

Judge Wilson asked the next day whether I had recorded the facts correctly and the offender said yes.

His explanation: "I have just come out of prison after years. I am scared of the outside and want to go back. At least they feed and give me a bed. "

The Judge obliged and put him back into prison for another eighteen months,

7

Theory and reality didn't always connect.

It was a lovely Sunday afternoon shift in Hamilton and the city was in a relaxed mood. In the middle of the city was a small lake. Hamilton city was inland, and the Waikato River meanders through this docile rural community. The river was not very safe for swimming and hence the safe lake was a popular spot for families. Many little yachts sail backwards and forwards hunting for the next wisp of wind. At one end of the lake was a café/kiosk and children's playground. On this particular Sunday, one of the local radio stations was holding a fun event and large crowds were gathered.

One of the favourite spots for young swimmers was a slide going into the lake. The lake was not very deep and parents have very little fear for the safety of their children.

Scotty and I were on patrol. We decided to cruise around the lake and walk amongst the crowd as a public relations exercise. We had no expectation of any crime or incidents, as the chances are remote of anything untoward happening. We parked our patrol car, put our caps on and started to wander through the crowds. It was pleasant with the sun warming the body, friendly conversations and little children running up to say hello to the Policemen.

The lake had large numbers of black swans and ducks swimming amongst the children, all enjoying the day together. Scotty comments that there was a crowd gathering at the slide area and so we started to wander towards the crowd. Our expectation was the radio station doing something special for the kids.

"Constables came quickly," a distraught woman yells to us. She was running from the crowd towards us. We sped up our walking pace but looking cool and relaxed was important, so we did not break into a run. Then we hear the crowd talking about a body. Maybe it was time to break into a run. We couldn't afford to run too fast as we did not know what we were going to and Policemen running gets everyone looking and can cause panic.

Another member of the public yells at us that there has been a drowning. To hell with cool, there was a life at risk. We both sprinted towards the crowd. We pushed our way through and lying on the concrete pad at the slide was a little limp body. Everyone was just standing around, looking. Neither of us talked.

Scotty was straight down over the body and started mouth-to-mouth resuscitation. I started CPR and used my portable radio to call for an Ambulance. Suddenly the crowd was giving us a ton of advice. We are not doing the procedure correct. We should be doing this or that. It was too much, and I swore at them that if they knew so much, why nobody was doing anything when we arrived. My comments worked and we had silence.

The silence splintered with the distant sound of an Ambulance siren. The sound was of angels winging their way to save the day.

Scotty and I were perspiring heavily. There was no sign of life from the little child. We couldn't stop.

Helplessness!

Worry!

Anxiety!

I yelled at a guy in the crowd to meet the Ambulance and get them to us as quickly as possible. The man scurried off over to the roadside.

The little child was lifeless. We continue with the mouth-to-mouth and CPR. Scotty refused to change roles. I looked across towards the road and saw the civilian running back towards us with two Ambulance Officers in tow.

The Ambulance Officers arrived with their equipment and took over from us. Next thing the shift Sergeant arrived to check out what was happening. Scotty and I both knew the Ambulance Officers; we had attended other incidents with them in the past. Eventually the senior one of the two looked up at us and said it was over.

The Ambulance agreed to take the body to the nearby Hospital for a Doctor to certify death and we can take over from there. We loaded the limp little body onto the stretcher and took it towards the waiting Ambulance. As we got near, Scotty dived into a bush and started vomiting. Scotty had a young child at home the same age as the one we could not resuscitate. It was all too personal for him. Once the body was in the Ambulance, I spoke to the Sergeant and he agreed Scotty should go home. I was more than happy to do all the procedures and paperwork on my own.

The four-year old child had fallen into the lake and none of the other children noticed until one stood on the body. No one knows how long the child had been in the water. The mother had gone to get an ice cream and did not realise her child was close to the water. She was understandably distraught.

Epilogue: Scotty returned to work the next day and carried on as normal. The theory was that Police switch off their emotions and cope. Some incidents, such as this was for Scotty, are impossible as the emotions get under the armour of your uniform and inflict emotional pain. Scotty had two young children at the time of this incident but went on to have a family of four kids.

At the Coroner's hearing, I complained about the lack of rescue services available at the lake, but officialdom stayed silent.

8

Love at first sight

Early in my Police career, while on the beat in Wellington, a burglar on premises necessitated Police Dog Thor attending and capturing the offender. I was mesmerised. Thor was a handsome bugger and his handler, Des, a real cool dude. I chatted with Des later in the night and this was when I resolved to become a Dog Handler.

When stationed at Hamilton, in my off-duty time I would go out with the Dog Handlers - especially on Wednesday, training day. I played the offender so the dog could track me, or hide so it could find me, or better still, wear the padded sleeve so they could practise their "man work." I loved every second of it and could not wait for the next time to do some more.

I applied for first vacancy that came up and my mate Fred got it. I was ecstatic for him because we were kindred spirits. The next vacancy I missed out again to a guy who had never shown any interest in the dogs. I was totally gutted. The department put down the regulation concrete pad and shifted a dog kennel in. He was to go to a course in a few weeks. I could not look him in the eye at the station - he had my kennel and got my dog.

One evening at home the phone rang and it was Fred. He advised me that the current Handlers threatened a mass resignation unless I got the next pup. The hierarchy overturned their decision and I was to join my old patrol buddy as a Dog Handler. Sleep was absent that night as my mind raced with the excitement of what lay ahead.

The next morning the duty inspector rang and officially told me the news. I was to leave for the training college within two weeks.

Arriving at the Police Dog College at Trentham, my mind and body dealt with every imaginable emotion every few seconds, excitement, fear, nervousness, elation, awe and anticipation. I had dogs all my life and now I was to learn formally how to train one. A piece of blotting paper waiting for the ink spillage.

I had never been to the Police Dog College and did not know what to expect. We arrived in a Police minivan. Down the driveway the tall gum trees by the 8-foot fence line, with all the training jumps in the paddock outside of the fence, had my heart racing. There were six of us from all over New Zealand. The New Zealand flag flapping around the flagpole at the entrance set a formal tone.

We all mustered in the classroom. I was eyeing the others up - the competition to be the best already brewing in my gut. It was explained that there were five pups in the kennels and one slightly older dog. The instructors did a big sales pitch that this was the best young dog they had ever seen. We were to go out to the kennels and if we could all agree on our "pup" then that was great. If we could not, then the cages would be numbered, and we would draw a number. Four of the selections were bitches and I was keen to have a bitch. The pups were four months old, and still balls of fluff.

Out we all went and the one the instructors were trying to "sell" got the most attention. I wandered along all the kennels and at the end was this little black bitch - she was 100% black. The only other colour was this delightfully slobbery pink tongue. She got extremely excited at seeing me and it felt like she was picking me, rather than the other way around. I went into her kennel, which was a large fenced-in run with a bed at the end. We just felt like kindred spirits. It was a no-brainer for me. Trouble was brewing amongst the other Handlers as they argued over this special dog. There was no way there was going to be agreement. Dogs were going to be allocated by draw. I argued that I did not need to be involved in the draw as no one else was interested in the one I wanted. Oh, the fun of belonging to a disciplined organisation. I had no votes and had to go into the draw. I drew the middle one of the numbers and got my little black beauty. It felt like a relationship made in heaven. I could not wait to go out to her. We were allocated ten minutes to get to know our dog and then came back in with what name we might want to call them. The hierarchy had the final say in whether our name was acceptable. This was "C" litter, so all names had to start with that letter.

My first choice was Carla but rejected without any explanation. My second choice was Cara, which was accepted, and so started our career together. Now the journey of fifteen months training to get her "operational" began.

Most of the puppy course was in the classroom. The pups still required a lot of sleep. We received instruction in the feeding, grooming, exercise and socialisation regimes we needed to work on before coming back to our next one-month course.

As part of the socialisation training, we took the pups to Upper Hutt for walks amongst the public to get used to normal street noises. This was their first time away from the college. They were in collars with their leads, so over exuberant trainee Handlers would not be too tough.

We were in Upper Hutt walking Indian file along the footpath. It was Cara and my turn to lead the walk. From my perspective, she was still a cuddly, slobbery ball of fluff. Coming towards us was an old lady, bent over on a walking stick. My concern was Cara would want to jump up and lick her. Instead, she went to the end of the lead and went crazy barking at this lady. I had no idea what to do. Next thing "Taffy"-one of our instructors-was alongside me quietly giving me instructions to get Cara calmed down and past the old lady. I thought she was at risk of having a heart attack. Once past, Cara went back to bubbly puppy mode.

Taffy asked me to tell what I thought had happened. I could describe the scene, but the logic was missing for me. He gathered us all around and explained that from a dog's perspective the lady was in a threatening stance being bent over. Watch two dogs sizing each other up to determine whether to fight - they are hierarchal creatures, always looking for who was strongest/weakest. Dogs read body language and even as a little pup, it was pure instinct.

Back in the classroom they showed us a video on wild dogs in Africa and explained how everything we were going to train our dogs to do, they knew naturally. The difference was they were going to do it in relation to a command.

We had to have our pups well socialised, able to do basic obedience, and be fanatical retrievers when we came back for our next course in about ten months.

On returning to Hamilton station I was back on normal duties except shifts were now seven hours; one hour per day was for dog care and training.

Our back section was completely fenced and so I converted it into a dog-training compound. Training Cara was so much fun. She loved our time together, as she was out of the kennel with me. Therefore, our times involve much play, as well as serious times on training. She was so easy to train. When she got something right and got a lot of praise, she looked up with her smiling brown eyes and was pleased.

There was a primary school not far from our home, and with the blessing/permission of the Headmaster Cara goes to school at breaks to play with the kids. I often wondered whether the tail would fly off with so much wagging. She took it personally when the bell rang, and the kids had to go back into class. I got this look "what have we done wrong" as I put her lead on and walked her home.

Everything was going fantastic, except for one area - she refused to retrieve. She had no interest in the regulation wooden dumbbell - I tried tennis balls and everything - she just refused to run out and get them.

We were within two weeks of the next course and she still would not retrieve. Her obedience work was pretty to watch. She did the heel with her tail wagging and looking up at me for approval. It was picture perfect.

I saw our career coming to a rapid halt because I couldn't get her to retrieve. I left the dumbbell on the ground and was beside myself. In frustration I kicked the thing as hard as I could, and next thing this black bullet zooms past me and grabbed the dumbbell. I let out whoops of joy and praised her as much as I could. She smiled at me and then we had a game of chase, her running with the dumbbell and me chasing. When we left for the course she was at a point where she almost cartwheeled at the sight of her dumbbell. I went to Trentham in a very happy state.

On the one-month course, we started to teach our youngsters how to track. Cara was a natural and she knew when she tracked well and I was happiest.

When we returned to Hamilton, I was a full-time trainee Dog Handler until we got operational. Life couldn't get any better. Cara was top at obedience and her tracking ability in all sorts of conditions was going in leaps and bounds. The training tracks were getting harder, in both length and time after laying the track. The future boded well.

Finally, we got back to the College for our last two-month course. Part of the course involved doing dog displays for visiting schools. The competition between us Handlers was intense, even though we all got on well. When the school children were lined up against the fence we would stand out of the ground with our dogs on our left and when we were introduced we took one step forward and the dog was meant to come forward the one step and go straight back into the sit position. On one occasion, Cara and I were the last ones introduced. As the introductions started at the other end of the line, I slipped my boot under the dog next to me and started to rub his "tummy." Being a male dog, he got over aroused and as they step forward to be introduced, he ejaculated over the parade ground.

"Taffy" was doing the commentary and when the children asked why that dog was doing what it was, he replied that it was a secret command to get the dog doing aerobic exercise. It cost me a dozen of beer as a fine, but worth it.

Graduation day came. Our course finished at the same time as a recruit wing and so we dressed up in formal Uniform and dogs in formal Police coats paraded with the recruits and shared their ceremony. Cara and I were both so proud of graduating and then we wanted to get to the real work and show how good we were in reality.

9

You never forget the first

The job was to prove ourselves on "the street."

The area we had not mastered well on the course was to leave an offender once attacked. I figured that on the job training would fix the problem. I was confident of a good career as Cara was one of the best tracking dogs on the course.

My first week was day shifts and more training. I wanted to get into real dog work. The first night shift was uneventful and still no "catch" to our name. The second night shift we had a few jobs, but they came to nothing. By the time Saturday night came around, I started getting despondent.

A patrol called in that trouble was brewing at a hotel in the main street, Victoria Street. This was not a real job for the dog, but I decided to attend. Three patrol cars in attendance when I arrived, and they were at the south end of the melee. I parked at the northern end. Cara technically knew crowd control so here was an opportunity to put her to the real test. I got her out of the van and put her into a double click chain The double click stops the choke chain impact and strangling.

The objective was for her to fan in front of me on a short lead, snapping and growling at the crowd to make them move.

It took a bit of work to get Cara into frenzy and then she was roaring at the crowd. If worked properly a dog can clear as many as it would normally take ten staff. Cara was doing her stuff. I saw a couple of Detectives in the middle of the crowd, both of whom I had worked with as street partners in the past. One of the patrols had made an arrest and put a prisoner in the back of their car. They didn't follow proper procedure; they failed to handcuff their prisoner and did not secure their vehicle. I was moving to the street side of the footpath, Cara frothing at the bit making an incredible noise. I looked down the street and saw the prisoner get out of the patrol car and make a run for it. There were about fifty people between him and us.

I had no idea what would happen if I released Cara and then I realised all my colleagues were looking at me expectantly. Blast! Not how I wanted my first incident to unfold. I ran onto the road and had Cara facing towards the direction of the escapee. In these circumstances, I was not obliged to yell a warning, which was just as well because too many questions about Cara's performance are racing through my mind. Off came the lead quickly followed by the attack command. Cara pined her ears back and was after him. The chase was on. Adrenaline motors through the body. Then horror!

One of the Detectives had spotted the escapee and decided to chase him, unaware Cara was on her way. He ran out onto the road, well in front of Cara and started to put chase. Panic! I couldn't stop Cara and she was likely to attack the Detective. The world changed into slow motion.

Cara was bearing down on the Detective who was in her

direct line from the escapee. Without any warning she slowed her pace down and runs looking at the Detective and then swings wide to check out the front guy. I am silent. Cara accelerated past the Detective. She attacked the escapee. By the time I got there, she had started to tear his clothing. Quickly handcuffed and handed over to some very red-faced Constables.

The Detective told me he had no idea Cara was chasing the escapee and when he heard her coming, he did not know what to do. He figured he was at greatest risk if he stopped and so he continued. I really did not care as I had my first official catch and Cara had started her career.

10

Fire was terrifying

The speed with which it flays the tentacles of ruin sends
shudders through my spine.

Leaving Ngaruawahia from an incident, I was driving south
on the main highway to Hamilton. I did not have another
incident to attend and so no rush. At night when traffic was
light, the trip was pleasant. Cara was in the back resting and
even the Police radio was silent. The drive allows reflection
time without distraction. A lot of Police time was doing what
appeared to be nothing. In reality, my eyes never knew how
to stop, flicking from one scene to another. The training was
to look for anything out of the ordinary and it rarely let me
down.

It was a mild night and I knew the profile of the houses as I
had driven this road so often, going north to a variety of
incidents over the years.

My eyes explored to the right.

I flicked my head to the left again. The farmhouse had an eerie internal glow. The brain accelerated through a database of possibilities.

"Hamilton from Dogs: Can I have Fire in attendance north of Te Rapa by about 2 miles. A house fire! I will confirm if occupants are in the house." I reported.

I gunned the engine and the vehicle reacted. There was a gate just ahead and I slid the vehicle through the gate. My heart was racing with my mind, both trying to set new speed records. All I had was a small vehicle fire extinguisher in the back – waste of time. I braked hard, close to the front of the house.

The house was timber, with a corrugated iron roof and about fifty to sixty years old. The night light made it hard to recognise the beige exterior. This was an old farm homestead with a big ornate wooden veranda around the outside. The red/orange glow was coming from the lounge, but there was no smoke coming out of the chimney.

I sprinted to the front door. The solid wooden door with stained glass panels was beautiful. The timber was native New Zealand Kauri, used for sailing ship masts because of its strength. This was not the time to be admiring such things. I thumped the door bellowing "Police, wake up." There was no response. After a few minutes, I realised time was being wasted. Now the popping sound of an out of control fire reverberated through my ears. It was time to put my size eleven boots into action.

The training says: kick just above the lock. The first kick just bounced me off the door and I temporarily lost balance. The body jarred at the recoil. Another kick and bingo – the door flew open, with me losing balance and flying into the house.

"What the hell was going on!" shouted the dreary-eyed farmer. He staggered out of the bedroom in his white jockey underwear. He was medium build, with a tanned body reflecting years of working outside without a top on. My guess was he was in his late forties' early fifties. The weather-beaten face with wrinkles, night-time stubble, and evidence of years of hard physical work.

"Police – your house in on fire –get everyone out."

The farmer reacted with speed and advised me that only his wife and daughter were in the house. He went back into his bedroom to get his wife and I went into the hall. Smoke was pouring down the hall from the lounge and the fumes attacked my senses. My throat was drying up and eyes running. The rock and roll drums of the fire reverberated through my body. I talked to myself and kept calm but tried to balance the calm with speed. The door to my right might be a bedroom. I opened the door and went in fighting the urge to cough. To my right against the wall was a divan bed with a floral duvet.

Lying in the bed was a shape I assumed was the daughter. I rushed to the bed grabbing the bedding and yelled at her to get up. She woke with a start and screamed. The scream caused me to jump temporarily, before I composed myself again. I yelled that I was Police and she needed to get out. I saw a dressing gown draped on a nearby chair and grabbed it for her. Slowly coming into reality, she saw my uniform, stopped screaming and reacted. She must be about fifteen to sixteen years of age and slim build. She was in floral shorty pyjamas and to my relief appropriately covered.

The hallway was full of heavy rancid smoke.

"Keep bent over and as low as possible, below the smoke line," I spluttered trying to keep the amount of smoke going into my own lungs to a minimum.

I led her by the hand; we made our way to the front door and into fresh, beautiful, succulent clean air. Her parents were standing at the front of my dog van and we gathered. I called up to check Fire was on their way. For the first time I allowed myself to have a coughing fit.

The flames leapt through the windows, dancing with the night sky. The fire danced, performing to the stars, waltzing into further recesses of the house. The orange and red flames were contesting for dominance. Then I realised we were getting very hot – I told the family we needed to move further away. We heard the sirens trumpeting the rescue ballad, but it felt too late.

As the Fire truck came through the gate, the roof collapsed with thunderous applause. The noise exploded in the night silence. In less than fifteen minutes, there was nothing left for the Fire Brigade to deal to other than dampening down the hot spots.

My radio came alive and I left the family with the Fire Brigade to go off to attend the next incident.

****

I was at Te Rapa racecourse doing obedience training with Cara. It was a warm summer's night and a full moon. The Regional Police Dog trials were in a couple of months and I wanted to win. Winning the regionals allows us to compete in the National Police Dog trials. Every aspect of our work must be perfection. Cara and I had an outstanding record of accomplishment in the field, but nationals have proved elusive in the past – this was to be our year.

I had all the jumps in the spare kennel in the van. We practised all the normal obedience and I headed to the van to unload the jumps. Cara was in the "lie & stay" position. She had to be able to stay until commanded otherwise. She loved the jumps and I knew getting them out excited her, but this was a good discipline.

The van was facing towards the city when I came to the back of it. As I lowered the tailgate, my mind replayed what I had just seen. A thin plume of smoke rose above the Vardon Road shops. There should be no smoke from that direction as it was a residential area, just beyond the shops. Blow the jumps; this must be a house fire. I called Cara and she raced to me, into the back of the van and quickly locked in.

"Hamilton from Dogs: Can you dispatch Fire towards Vardon Road. I am trying to get an exact location but there is a house fire."

The previous fire haunted my mind and I remembered the speed with which that house burnt down. I had to find this one quickly. Our normal protocol with the racing club was we were to treat the grounds with respect. My tires spin as I gunned the van on the long grass, and it took a few moments to get traction. I drove out of the racing area and round the side of the buildings to find the palm lined drive out of the racecourse.

Operations instructed me Fire was on their way and did I have a more precise location.

Not yet!

The van slid right onto Te Rapa Road. The smoke, previously hidden by the tall palms on the driveway peeks across rooftops, teasing me. I flew down the road and through the traffic lights. My window was down so I use my sense of smell as well. Teasing me over my big nose was a way of life, but this night my trumpet was invaluable. At least the smoke did not appear to be getting any worse. It was coming from a Unit down a driveway. A Unit does not have a fireplace, so this was definitely another house fire. I radioed in the address and parked on the road, as I knew my vehicle would be in the way of the coming Fire Engine.

I scampered down the driveway with a tall wooden fence either side. I heard the crackling of the fire and this means it was gathering momentum. The brick Unit was small and had a little concrete patio with double ranch sliders giving entry to the Unit. I saw the flames in the room. Inside lying on the sofa was a man. I grabbed the handle and luckily, the door opened. I knew oxygen was bad for a fire, but I needed access to this bloke. He had a single blanket across him, and I didn't know whether he was conscious or unconscious. I smelt the alcohol over the smoke, how the fire probably started makes sense.

On the floor beside the sofa was a full ashtray. My guess was the bloke was mid-late twenties. He had a T-shirt and denim jeans. He had the air of a labourer about him and the physique to match.

There was not time for pleasantries. I grabbed him by the arm and forcefully pulled him off the sofa. The body came alive and takes a wild swing at me. I reacted in time, jumping back to avoid the inevitable. I yelled I am the Police and his Unit was on fire. He registered the gravity of the situation and semi calmed down. He staggered when he got to his feet; eye foot coordination was giving him a few problems. He turned to go back inside, and I grabbed his arm pulling him towards the outside.

He started a coughing fit, which I am not sure was from the fire smoke or his smoking. He told me his mate was inside in the first bedroom off the hall.

Above the growing noise of the fire, I heard the siren of hope. As we went across the patio, the smoke was too much and we both simultaneously broke into a massive coughing fit.

My lungs were on fire, my eyes stinging, but I had to go back in. I left him against the fence and rushed back towards the Unit. The flames were screaming through the ranch slider at me.

"Stay still, don't go in!" The voice carried an air of authority.

I turned around and see a Fireman with breathing apparatus rushing towards me. I advised him there was still another inside. Heroes die young. I heeded his advice and retire to let a couple of Fire Fighters go into the Unit. Others arrived with hoses and started spraying the Unit. It felt like eternity, but in reality, was less than a minute when they came out of the Unit with the second occupant, naked.

It did not take them long to get the blaze under control. I left the occupants with the Fire Fighters and carried on my sojourn into the night. We didn't go back to try to finish our obedience training, as my adrenaline was slightly high.

11

A school burglary with a large twist

Cara lived at home as a friendly family pet when she was not working, but once she was on duty, we are both professional. A huge part of our success meant we understood each other, and to develop that level of trust requires hundreds of hours training every year. Cara, like all dogs, had her unique personality; exuberant, brave, determined and focussed.

Cara almost didn't make it to graduation, simply because of her small size.. She made up for her stature with her work ethic and attitude. The area of her work she loved the most was tracking. Cara was an easy dog to read when tracking. On a fresh track, her head was high, ears standing proud and her nose sniffing with eager anticipation. The older the track, the lower her head and often I could estimate how far behind an offender we were by the height of her head. There awere very few occasions when I struggled to read what she was doing.

Night shift was when we got the most action.

"Hamilton to Dogs. Burglary at Huntly College tuck shop – alarm activation and offender seen running away."

"Roger."

Cara was standing up in her kennel behind me and when I answer the radio, she looked through the glass divider at me to check out whether we are about to go into action. I spun the steering wheel to do a U-turn and by the time we were facing the other direction, Cara was down in the foetal position behind me. She stayed in that position until she received signals from the vehicle and me that we were approaching the scene of whatever crime she was to solve. I activated the flashing lights and we proceeded across Hamilton city, watching out for other drivers who were sleepy or worse, drunk. My mind flashed back to the night I was rushing up Angelsea Street and there was a car ahead of me signalling a left turn. I had my flashing lights on going to an incident. Without warning, the car suddenly turned right in front of me and we had two severely damaged cars. I didn't want a repeat of that tonight.

Except for Ngaruawahia township, the rest of the trip was at maximum speed. The traffic was light so there was next to no delays or slow down periods on the trip. We came into the southern end of Huntly, turned off at the petrol station, and drove over the Waikato River Bridge. A right turn and we came to the school. I'd been here before and knew where the tuck shop was. Cara, realising the van was slowing down and I was talking on the radio stood up again to keep watch. Her head bent one side to the other as she tried to work out what we were attending.

I left her in the van at this stage until I could work out what had happened.

The school caretaker was waiting for us. He was dressed in

his winter pyjamas with an old woollen dressing gown, which looked as old and tatty as he did. He had his usual cigarette dangling in the side of his mouth.

"Bruce, saw the little bugger run off towards the River," he spluttered followed by a smoker's hacking cough. We had met on a number of previous occasions.

"How long ago and how many?"

"I rang straight away and only one," was his response.

I calculated that the offender had a twenty to thirty-minute start on us. I jogged back to the van and opened the back door, grabbing the lead off the hook just inside the door. As I grabbed the lead with my right hand, I slipped the bolt to Cara's cage with the other. She didn't hesitate as she flew past me. I then found the tracking harness and called her back. Cara preferred the freedom of free tracking, but the bosses didn't like us doing this technique unless I could justify the urgency. Instead of free tracking, Cara was in her tracking harness, which had a thirty-foot line.

Cara was impatient. She found the scent and wanted to get started. She gave me a filthy look for slowing things down – she knew the harness means we operate at my speed, not hers. I reminded her she was useless at reading the law books at training school and therefore had to trust my judgement on such matters.

Cara's tail was high and so was her head, so the track was nice and fresh. We started to move away from the tuck shop and then without warning Cara swung to the left and started tracking again. I had never seen her react like this before and could understand what was happening. She tracked a few feet and then rushed to her right and appeared to start tracking afresh. Then the same thing happened again, this time way out to my left. She tracked for a few feet, stopped and rushed over to my right. Progress was slow.

The Huntly patrol had been at another incident and called up on my portable radio to say they were on their way to assist. I was glad. Huntly is a coal mining town and a large number of the inhabitants are extremely fit and muscular. Cara and I had attended some very violent incidents in the past and I always liked knowing back up was never far away.

Cara was now tracking a width of nearly sixty feet, with one track about thirty feet to my left and another equal distance on my right. I rationalised that we had two to three offenders and she was trying to track them all at once. My dilemma was she was to select one track and stay with that one.

We were now heading away from the school and crossing the sports field. At the far side of the sports field was a large stop bank for the Waikato River. My guess was the offender(s) would go over the stop bank, so they were out of sight, and then walk their way home. We were gradually moving towards the stop bank. I decided not to make an issue of Cara working all the tracks for fear that she might get annoyed with me and not bother to track at all.

We eventually got to the stop bank and Cara was making her way up. I was right behind her, rather than the normal thirty feet (this was not a normal track). As we came over the brow of the stop bank, I saw people everywhere. To our right, about one hundred feet away, right beside the river was a fire. At this stage, it was impossible to guess how many people were around the area.

"Cops" yelled a voice and suddenly there were bodies heading in all directions.

"Stop or I'll release the dog," I shouted. Cara read the moment and started frantic barking. They all stopped.

"Get over here by me and no one will be bitten," I ordered. Amazingly the sheep going into the slaughterhouse, with heads hung low, all sauntered their way in front of me and sat down on the grassy bank. I radioed the Huntly patrol where we were and asked them to join me.

"Dogs from Hamilton, situation update please."

"Roger, we have just apprehended seventeen youths and are taking them into custody."

We walked the offenders back by the route I had come, over the bridge and through to the Huntly Police Station – Cara made sure none of them got out of step. One turned to me and said, "Your dog could only have caught one of us and you another." I pointed out the error in his logic because we had successfully caught seventeen.

12

A disturbed rugby test

Quiet nights kept us on edge the most, because the quietness has a history of deception. There was an international Rugby test on TV in the middle of the night. The duty Senior Sergeant "borrows" a TV for his office.

I followed my father's footsteps and did my time as a Rugby referee, but only for a short time. Rugby is a religion in New Zealand, way outstripping the main Churches with devotees. An international test was compulsory viewing. The Senior Sergeant and I quipped about the quiet night and our speculation it would erupt and there would be no chance of watching the game. We were half-right.

At 0515hrs on 16th November 1980, the call came in on the 111-emergency line. A farmer out the back blocks of Huntly called in to say a car had crashed into the fence below his house and the occupants had run off. Earlier in the night, Huntly Police reported a stolen car and the crashed one fitted the description. Even though there was a rugby match, and I was meant to finish work at 0500 hours, this sounded too good to be true.

I raced to the basement and fired the dog van into life.

Cara instantly fired up and was ready for action after a night with no activity. Technically, it was about a forty-five-minute drive to the scene, but for a Police Dog, seconds make a difference between success and failure. We arrived at the scene in less than forty-five minutes.

I knew Cara needed to relieve her bladder. A dog with a full bladder was as distracted as a human in the same predicament. On arriving at the scene, the local Huntly cop was talking with the farmer. The vehicle embedded in the fence. I opened the back of the van, let Cara out to go toilets, and went to talk to the farmer.

"Where did you last see them?" I enquired.

"See where your dog is going?" says the farmer pointing at Cara.

Full bladder or not, Cara found the track and was off. Technically, she was supposed to be in her tracking harness, but the fresh track allowed her to operate at her own pace. It was also clear the offenders had a considerable start and to catch them required speed on our part. Cara loved tracking and the body language reflected her passion. The black tail wagged furiously. Rural tracks like this were heaven.

The area was undulating hills and there was a reasonable length of grass in the paddocks, keeping the scent fresh. The only slight distraction was multiple offenders. The dog tracks the freshest human scent and when there are multiple offenders, it was hard for them to work out which one to follow. To be successful the dog selects a particular scent and stays with that one.

The track started to follow the road, but one paddock in from it. I was running as hard as I could to keep up with her. Cara flew over the fences with great ease and just kept going. The fences slowed me up, as I didn't fancy the barbed wire giving me a vasectomy at this stage in life. Next, we crossed towards the road and then over. These offenders knew where they are going – they had to be locals.

Cara went up a steep hill and down the other side. I decided to stay on the ridge and follow her from the vantage point. I knew Cara would track for hours and I was the weak link in time. Up and down hills at a running pace, in heavy army style regulation boots often wore me out. The boots are essential for 95% of the work, but occasionally such as this, running shoes would make a significant difference.

We tracked down by a small lake and around the edge. Cara wasn't missing a beat and her tail wagging was in time with the excitement. The track turned to our right and we crossed the road again. The Huntly Police car was cruising with the objective of slowing the offenders down to give us more of a chance. The patrol car used their spotlight to keep track of our movement, and usually involved curses from me for having a bright light in my eyes. There was no portable radio communication in this area –it was dead, and I didn't have mine with me.

Cara swung back towards the road and then we were tracking along the side of it. I heard a car coming towards us and worried about Cara not being in her harness. She concentrated so hard she never noticed anything around her. The car was not moving fast and then it came around the corner and the headlights blinded me. They were on full beam. It was the farmer. He pulled alongside.

"Jump in mate I'll take you back to your vehicle. They are long gone."

I thanked the farmer and rejected his kind offer. Even though he was used to working dogs, understanding the dynamics of a Police Dog was different. If I pulled Cara of a "hot track", it would take hours of training to get her back up to speed. When Cara was tracking, I followed her no matter what.

"I think you're crazy mate, but your choice." He retorted.

A few moments later we crossed another fence and Cara headed down the hill into a bit of a gully. I stuck to my pattern of staying on the ridge top – less distance for me. The sun was rising and hit me in the tired eyes. Cara was speeding up. This was a sure sign that she was getting closer. I decide to leave the ridge and join her. The pace was taking its toll on me and I started retching. Cara was not missing a beat, so my discomfort was meaningless. Cara's performance inspired me to ignore my body, which was pleading for rest.

And then!

Cara was starting to raise her head. This meant she was wind scenting the offender(s) instead of tracking. Cara went through some bush and as I burst out the other side, she caught one offender. I quickly applied handcuffs and took him back to the road with Cara doing her usual assistance tricks to make sure he did not try to run again. As we got to the road, luck was on our side. The Huntly patrol car was there. I handed over the prisoner and asked for some temporary (plastic) handcuffs. I stuffed a few sets in my pocket and took Cara back to the spot where we caught this guy. Cara instantly picked up the track again and was flying.

My body was arguing as hard as it could, but I knew we were close to catching more. A few more bushes and we caught another couple. They stopped when they heard their mate yell at Cara's interview technique. They quickly gave themselves up, were handcuffed and taken to the patrol car. I knew we still had one outstanding.

Cara quickly picked up the last track; even she was showing signs of fatigue. The level of concentration was tiring even for an extremely fit Police Dog. We went through light scrub and I heard running footsteps ahead. I called on him to stop to no avail. Then Cara and I were in a clearing and the last offender was only yards ahead of us. He picked up a nearby large rock to take Cara on.

"Feel free mate, it will only aggravate her more and your wounds will be worse." I warn.

Luckily, he saw reason and put the rock down. Cara just flops where she was. The offender has no idea of our state of exhaustion. He was taken to the Huntly patrol car which transported all prisoners.

Cara jumped in the boot of the patrol car to travel back to the dog van. The farmer obliged with a cup of tea and a large bowl of water for Cara.

The official commendation we got reads in part:

The Constable and his Dog actually followed a track over both country and road surfaces for a distance of eight kilometres before finally catching the offenders." The distance was further because of the cross-country nature of the track. The road distance was eight kilometres. From a Dog Handler perspective, this was our finest.

13

Drunks are not as charming as they think!

It was Saturday night and Hamilton city slumbers in the early morning hours. Traffic was light and from a Policeman's perspective, any traffic was suspect for moving about in the early hours. Night shift was my favourite because as a Dog Handler you have the best action. Night also brings out the weird and wonderful.

As the night shift Dog Handler, I spent quiet time in the central part of the city. I was driving south along the main street, Victoria Street, and as I cruised past Ward Street, I saw a light-coloured sedan vehicle driving toward me. In itself this was not a spectacular matter, except Ward Street was a one-way street and this car was driving the wrong way.

I couldn't ignore the vehicle, even though traffic work was not the role of a Dog Handler. I spun the dog van around and turned on the flashing lights. I went into Ward Street, coming from the correct direction and almost had a head on collision with the other vehicle. Remembering my French lessons from school, I spoke aloud inside my vehicle challenging the parenting of the opposing driver. I started to turn around to go after this vehicle when I saw in my mirrors the car was turning around. I stopped and waited. Next thing the other vehicle was alongside me and I got my first look at the driver. He looked to be in his late teens, reasonably tidy hair and not our usual looking criminal. I realised he did not notice me. He had a vacant expression, just staring ahead.

I drove alongside of him and waved at him to pull over. I blasted the horn. No reaction! Another blast. Again, no reaction! I drove in front of him and started to force him off the road. He eventually hit the curb, and something inside his pea brain registered and he stopped the car. I made sure my vehicle kept him wedged in.

I wandered back to his vehicle and the young driver just sat there looking straight ahead. I had a right one here.

"Driver, get out of the vehicle."

There was no change in the situation, so I grabbed the driver's door and opened it. The scene unfolded in slow motion. His body gradually started to tilt out the door and then its own weight and gravity did the rest. I looked down at my feet to this crumpled looking young man.

"Alright smart arse, get on your feet!"

The body was not moving. Frustrated I made my second mistake. I picked him up and leant him against his car. His eyes were not looking at me; they were not registering anything. I was just about to speak to him again, when without any warning his mouth erupts with hot, disgusting smelling vomit. I was directly in the path of the torrent and it happened with such speed I couldn't avoid the showering that followed. I jumped back to avoid the second onslaught and in doing so let go off him. In the movies, the next piece would be hilarious but in reality, it was not amusing. In slow motion, he slumped to the road again vomiting all the way down with an incredible techno-coloured vomit. It was fascinating how carrots and sweet corn keep their shape in the digestive tract.

"You bastard!"

I went back to my dog van to get a breath test kit. Whether I wanted to or not I now had to start the drink drive procedure. At least he was going nowhere and was keeping himself warm by lying in his vomit. I muttered under my breath about what I think about drunks and their behaviours.

I came back with an assembled breath test device.

"I require you to blow into the device with one long breath, and not stop until I tell you so."

There was no way I was picking him up off the street, so I put the device in his mouth. This time I prepared and jumped out of the way just in time as another spray erupted.

"You have failed a breath test and I now require you to accompany me to the Police Station for the purposes of a second breath test and possibly a blood test."

I had to go through all the legal jargon in case he remembered something I did wrong and we ended up in court. There was no way I was going to get another patrol car to come and transport him to the station, as their vehicle would fill with vomit. Therefore, I half dragged, half carried him to my van and strapped him into the front passenger's seat. He duly obliged by throwing up across the dash. Earlier in my career, I had helped an Ambulance crew stomach pump a man who had alcoholic poisoning and I knew the human body was capable of great volumes.

"Dogs to Hamilton, returning with one suspect drunk driver. Can someone meet me out front and help me carry him in?"

The youth was not under arrest at this stage so by law I had to bring him in through the front doors. The Duty Senior Sergeant met me at the front of the Police Station.

"I had to come out myself. I don't recall a Dog Handler ever doing a drunk driver. Do you know what you are doing?"

Then he looked at my uniform.

"Let's get him in the medical room quickly."

The cleaners were going to love us later in the night as he vomited twice in the fifty-yard walk to the medical room. The Senior Sergeant was on one side of him and me the other. When we got into the medical room, we sat him in a chair. In slow motion, he slid out of the chair. We put him back on the chair and it happened again. Moreover, a third time it happened.

"Bugger this" said the Senior Sergeant, "we'll do him under the old provisions where two of us can certify him drunk. Let us put him into a drunken cell now. See if the Police Doctor will come and if he does not want to don't worry."

The drunken cell was just a concrete room with a big soak hole in the middle, for cleaning. There was no toilet, nothing in the way of furniture so prisoners can harm themselves. As we turned to walk away, the young offender vomited again.

I went out to the dog van and got a spare Uniform – time for a shower to clean up. After the shower I tried to contact his next of kin – he had his driver's licence and he was only sixteen.

"Hello, Mr XXX, this is Constable Howat of Hamilton Police. I have arrested your son for drunk driving."

The father was irate. "My son does not drink. I am coming to the station to get my son and lay a complaint against you." He told me I was on a power trip and this was harassment.

The father arrived twenty minutes later. The Senior Sergeant and I took him down to the extremely smelly cell containing his son. The Senior Sergeant and I winked at each other. We stood either side of the son and slightly to the rear as we picked him up making sure we aimed his mouth at the father. The son displayed his finest pyrotechnics display of the night, all over his father's lovely pin stripe suit. The father was wild.

"Your son will be staying in custody until court on Monday morning," said the Senior Sergeant using the most formal tone he could muster. There was no argument.

****

On the Monday morning court appearance, the Judge remanded the young offender in custody because he was too drunk to be able to plead. A Police Doctor examined him on the Sunday for fear of alcoholic poisoning.

14

Even dogs need their sleep

I attended a function with my brother and one of his friends, Tom who was boasting about a fantastic guard dog he owned. According to him, there are many house burglaries in his area and protection of his family was important. The house burglary situation was news to me, but I only work for the Police and didn't know this problem area. In this discussion, I kept quiet, on the outside, as my inner head remembers the hundreds upon hundreds of hours spent in training Police Dog Cara and our experience. Even when operational, every day I spent at least twenty to thirty minutes grooming Cara and a minimum of one hour on training exercises. In my mind, I was very cynical about how good Tom's guard dog was in reality.

About two months after the conversation with Tom I attended a prowler complaint in the Enderby suburb of Hamilton. The complainant heard a crashing noise in his back yard and curious he went outside in time to watch a "shape" disappear over his wooden fence. The house was a standard New Zealand weatherboard one, concrete driveway up the side to a tin garage at the rear. The painted house was traditional white, with the colour determined on the windowsills. The usual five-foot timber fence protected the house from invaders.

Cara and I arrived at the scene. She always checked which equipment I took out of the van because for her that was a clue as to what was going to happen next. I put her choke chain over her neck and grabbed the leather tracking harness hanging in the back of the van. Our next step was to go and talk to the complainant and find where he last saw our "offender." I was not interested in the details, as an incident car would get those. I wanted the information as to where to start tracking as quickly as possible. Time was precious to a dog and handler team. This was not the time for small talk; I wanted to get started.

Cara was in the down position beside me while I talked to the complainant. Her jet-black tail was wagging with anticipation and she raised her shiny head to try to air scent. She knows by me having the tracking harness what was going to happen next. I stood her up to prepare for tracking and put her between my legs as I took the choke chain off her neck. If I didn't hold her, she would just take off and start working. The lead and choke chain were tied around me for ease of carrying while tracking. Cara was fidgety; she hated the delays and just wanted to start her work. Her tail thumped against me as I quickly slipped her harness on. As soon as the last strap was connected, she knew I would release her, and she instantly started casting around for the freshest human scent.

Cara knew the limits of the system; connected to the tracking harness on a thirty-foot rope. She cast at a racing pace; for her the fun starts once she finds a track. Her tail was high, wagging with enthusiasm and her nose was sucking air through to differentiate all the different smells until she located the right one. She was so determined she almost cart wheeled when she hit the scent. It was always comical to watch as she found a fresh scent, as her first reaction was one of amazement. Cara had to decide which way was forward on the track and she only had a few seconds to make that critical decision. We didn't want to go back to where the offender came from; we wanted to go forward to where he/she might be now.

The darkness was our friend. Cara being jet black merged into the night. She was fast and silent. We flew over the fence with ease and Cara was onto a strong track. We quickly crossed the neighbour's property and then over their boundary fence. Cara had her head high, indicating the scent was strong and easy for her to follow. My size eleven boots were harder to keep quiet than her nicely padded paws. We both loved catching offenders unaware; they have not heard or seen us coming and this track had indications we might have another catch on our hands.

After four more properties, arriving at a higher fence, Cara was poised to go over six-foot-high walls with ease and she did not miss a beat. The training of Cara works a treat for her, but no one thought to train me how to climb such barriers silently and how to cross quickly. I made more noise than I liked crossing this particular fence and as I fell down on the other side, I watched Cara jump over this dog sleeping in the driveway. I scrambled to my feet and jumped over the same motionless dog. Obviously, the offender had done the same.

Cara was getting ahead of me, even though attached through the tracking line. I started to pull her back in so I could catch up. She hated slowing down but knew what was going to happen next. Her tail was wagging so hard I wondered if it would disconnect. When I finished reeling her in, I unclipped the rope from the harness so she was free to track at her own pace.

Across through the back of a few more properties she raced along and then out onto a side street. Suddenly she was circling, indicating she had lost the track. The obvious answer was the offender had some sort of vehicle at this point.

I called up the patrol car that was in the area and advised them what had happened. They followed up with the enquiry work. I had a game and played with Cara as a reward for her good work. After a few minutes of play, we started the walk back to our van. We didn't go through the back of the properties, but rather walked along the street.

As we walked along the footpath, playing a game together, me grabbing her tail and she spinning around pretending she was going to bite me. After doing that once she kept a watchful eye on me as we danced down the street together. I remembered the dog in the driveway. Nothing special about the dog; this was not the first time we have tracked over a sleeping dog, but something about this one was made my mind spin.

The houses looked different from the street to the sight we saw when tracking through the back of properties. I then recognised where we were. I had only seen Tom's house from the road and sure enough when we got to his house, there on the driveway was the dog, still sound asleep.

I caught up with Tom a couple of weeks later.

"I went to a prowler complaint in your neighbourhood Tom." I mentioned.

"I heard the neighbours talking about it –did you catch him?"

"No a car was used."

"Where did the offender run through?"

I explained the track to Tom and the dog that was asleep in a driveway. He burst out laughing that someone's dog could sleep that heavy.

"My dog would never sleep that heavy," chortled Tom.

15

A stirred memory

"Granddad, how does a Police Dog find someone in a building? Do they sometimes get it wrong?" My Grandson prompted a memory.

****

In the 1970's burglar alarms were unreliable devices. The alarms frequently had a mind of their own as to when they would operate. The exceptions were golf club alarms – I have no memory of attending a false alarm at a golf club.

"Dogs; alarm activation, Lochiel Golf Course."

The right foot went down more heavily on the accelerator pedal and the dog van responded. Cara felt the change in speed dynamics and automatically curled into the foetal position in her kennel directly behind me. No flashing lights and no squealing tyres were used. A fast and silent approach always proves our most successful for catching offenders unawares.

"Dogs, key holder on the way, he will meet you by the sweeping left hander just before you arrive."

It was good to know the Operations room staff had briefed the key holder. Many a potential good catch had been ruined by an overzealous key holder rushing into alarm activation with no knowledge of the potential risks they can encounter.

I saw a car parked on the left just before the sweeping corner with its park lights activated and gently bought the van to a halt. Advising the key holder to follow me in and wait in his vehicle until I gave the signal that I needed his services. The tactic was to drive from this point on with no headlights operating and drive as silently as possible, again coming to a gentle halt. Burglars use all their senses as they are on a full adrenalin rush and high fear alert. There were a few high-quality professional burglars, but their handwriting (modus operandi) at a crime scene separated them from the average burglar.

Cara was standing up in the kennel. She read the change in approach and knew that she was going into action. I could see her face in the rear vision mirror; if you can describe a dog as smiling, she was. Cara lived for her work and she caught on as to what was required in nearly every situation. She knew we were in silent mode and even if she saw someone running, in this instance, she would not bark. The routine was the boss would quietly open the back door, reach in and slip open the bolt to her kennel while grabbing the lead hooked on the side of the cage. She was to get out of the van with minimal fuss and noise and then he would want her to scoot quickly around the outside of the building, checking for scent. Her behavioural patterns had developed over a long period of training sessions everyday of her life since she was a four-month-old puppy.

The routine went according to plan and Cara found a scent leading to a forced open window. I left her guarding the window and advised the key holder we had someone inside and he must stay in his vehicle no matter what happened. The window was easy access for both Cara and me. She went in first and automatically went around the first room checking everything. I open up a door that took us further into the Clubhouse. I was confident the offender was still on the premises. Cara had her nose very high indicating a lot of fresh scent. She was working every room at a fast pace; she knew she was close but could not find her offender. The next part to check was the toilets, first the female toilet block and then the males. All of the indication from Cara was the offender was somewhere, but we had not been able to pinpoint the exact spot. Cara hated failure as much as I do, and we always worked until we were successful.

We left the toilets and went into the retail part of the Clubhouse. Cara was less interested in this part, even though I enjoyed checking out all the various golf equipment. We had now been through the whole building and Cara would not leave. Her behaviour said our offender was still in here somewhere, but I was puzzled as to where. We had checked the whole premises and still didn't have an offender. I considered getting the key holder in but decided against it. I didn't want another human scent to risk confusing Cara. Part of our success relied on me thinking about her role in our relationship and making sure she had the space to be a professional Police Dog. I sat on a stool at the bar to relive our process through the Clubhouse. Cara meanwhile was still moving with speed around the building, which now had every door open to give her free range. I deliberately left all the doors open so if an offender tried to make a break for it, she had the best chance of success.

I decided to go back to the male toilet block, as that was where Cara seemed the most interested. She was already in there when I got back and was running around lifting her head up all the time. All the cubicles were open, but Cara kept hanging around one in particular. I couldn't make sense of her reaction – a small male toilet cubicle was no place to hide someone. Then Cara put her front feet on the toilet seat and appeared to be looking up. Then she barked.

I went into the cubicle with her. Above the toilet was a huge air vent going to the roof. I looked up and saw nothing. Cara was still barking and getting more agitated. As my eyes adjusted to the new light, right at the top of the air vent was our burglar. I still didn't know how he got up there, but he was using all his strength to wedge himself in and stop from falling. He had nothing to hold onto, it was brute strength holding him up. I told him to come down. I cannot repeat his answer to me.

I commanded Cara to stay and I am sure she was smiling again. I left to get the key holder

"Any chance of a cup of tea?"

He looked at me quizzically. I explained that Cara had caught our offender and she was negotiating with him to give himself up. The best thing we could do was stay calm and have a cup of tea. The key holder opened the front door to the Clubhouse, and we went to the kitchen. Cara's barking echoed throughout the building.

We were halfway through our cup of tea when a voice called out.

"Call the dog off and I will give myself up."

What a dilemma! The decision was whether to rush back in and make the arrest straight away or finish a nice cup of tea. It seemed rude not to finish the cup of tea as the poor key holder had gone to such trouble. I also reasoned it was best to get the Detectives on their way so I would not have to hold onto the prisoner for long. It was just good manners to do the right thing by the people who have not broken the law.

When all the tasks were completed, I went in and put Cara on her lead. I couldn't understand the strange language and names the burglar was calling us. As soon as she was on her lead, he dropped out of the vent and agreed to have handcuffs applied. Cara and I stayed professional until the Detectives collected their new prisoner. Then the two of us went onto the Golf Course and played a fun game of chasing each other. The game carried on until I was too puffed to do anymore. After every success, we celebrated this way. Cara loved the games and they kept her motivated.

****

I explained to my Grandson that a dog has a sense of smell that was over one thousand times stronger than a human sense of smell. The times when a dog got it wrong was usually because the human was not reading the   behavior of their dog correctly. A Police Dog and handler operate as one – each understanding the other's role and respecting the uniqueness each had that makes them a strong team. The teamwork develops over hundreds of hours of training. Throughout her whole working life, Cara rarely missed a day without some form of training.

16

Humour was about timing

The quiet night meant it was likely to get busy. The radio cackled.

"Te Awamutu off the air at XXX address executing a warrant."

Well this was no work for Police Dog Cara; we slowly cruised the streets of Hamilton. While patrolling my eyes never sat still as they scanned the scenery for anything out of the ordinary. My mind was busy asking itself questions.

A while later the radio burst alive with urgency and concern in the operator's voice.

"Dogs, an armed offender incident at Te Awamutu." The initial call was to get us mobile, not to provide us with extensive information.

My mind swung into action and the van surged into accelerated life as I applied force to the pedal. I didn't worry about the squealing tyres as the van flung us into a new direction. Cara, who was standing at the window doing her part in the observation role, dropped to the floor of the kennel and went into the foetal position. Cara did this, as some of these trips were fast and scary.

We were only minutes away from the Hamilton Central Police Station and I needed to pick up the regulation pistol and six bullets. I came to a rapid halt out front of the Police Station, rushing inside, going through the public area and leaping over the counter. The Senior Sergeant's office was off to one side and on the other side was the Operations room. I rushed in and he had the safe open. On his desk was the pistol, six bullets and the holster. Beside the pistol was the filled-out arms book. I quickly signed approval to carry a firearm and rushed out, jumping the counter again and on my way to Te Awamutu.

Cara was standing up but as she saw me rush back to the van, she went back into her protected position. When the boss rushed like this, the van flew through corners. I lived halfway between Hamilton and Te Awamutu, so I knew the road. The van quickly got to full speed and stayed there until I got to Ohaupo Township. I slowed down through the township. It took only a few minutes to get through then back to full speed until we arrived in Te Awamutu.

"Dogs, rendezvous point was Maber Motors."

"Roger!"

The rendezvous point confused me. I still had no idea what I was going to but knew the information would come in due course. My confusion was Maber Motors lay only a few hundred yards from the address where the Te Awamutu cop was executing his warrant. I knew as we went over the brow of the next hill we were going down into Te Awamutu. Maber Motors was at the bottom of the hill.

I bought the van to a gentle stop at Maber Motors and parked behind some of the for-sale cars. I went to the back of the van, quickly and quietly let Cara out. There was a paddock next door and she hadn't had a toilet break for a while. She quickly did her business on command. Cara responded to my voice commands, but also to hand signals. I used hand signals to control her as we were only a few hundred metres from our suspected scene. Cara sensed something big and quickly slipped back into the van without fuss.

I watched up the road for anything out of the ordinary. A short while later the other members of the squad arrived. They were dressed in the Armed Offenders jersey, beret and special trousers that tuck into their boots. The blackened badges on the beret do not reflect any light, but still formally identify us as Police.

Phil the Detective Inspector in charge of the squad briefed us. Constable XX went to execute a warrant on XXX. He went into the house and now the person XXX was holding Constable XX at gunpoint. The parents rang the emergency number and provided us with our information.

We all looked at each other. This was a Policeman's worst nightmare; one of our own held hostage.

Our section was to go behind the Motels, directly opposite the house. Peter was the covering rifleman. I enjoyed working with Peter. He was a former Dog Handler. I used to go out with him on my days off to help with the training of his dog. I would lay tracks, hide in buildings or put the padded sleeve on for man work training. Peter was a happy person, always smiling and laughing. He was unique for seeing the funny side of any serious situation.

Normally we were emotionally detached from our work in armed incidents. This incident was different; one of our own was at gunpoint. My stomach was tight, and I knew the local cop well, adding to the inner tension I felt. All four of us in our section sneaked off through the back yard of Maber Motors and silently moved through the back of properties until we came to the Motels. We moved in single file with a gap between us, so one shot could only get one cop. We decided to go up the path on the right of the Motels as this put us in a direct line with the front of the house. The risk was someone in the Motels seeing us; it was a risk worth taking.

When we got to the path, we went down on all fours and kept close to the outside of the Motel Units. We took great care to make no noise with our boots.   Peter was directly in front of me and we moved in silence. Peter was just going past a kitchen window of a Unit when it suddenly opened.

"What are you doing?" challenged a female voice.

Peter did not look up.

"Police, cup of tea, milk and two sugars please."

The window closed and we heard voices inside the Unit. A few moments later, the window opens again and out came the cup of tea.

"And what about your mates" she asked.

I was fighting hysterics. Only Peter was capable of this.

"Anyway, what are you doing?" she enquired.

Peter told her we are the Armed Offenders squad and we had an incident across the road. It might pay to stay inside until it was over. He would bring back the empty cup later. We continued to move forward, in silent mode while Peter drunk his tea. He never spilt a drop; he placed the cup and saucer on the footpath by the final Unit.

Peter's action released a lot of tension for us all, even though we did not get a cup of tea.

The arrest of the offender was without any shots fired. Peter returned the empty cup and saucer to the woman in the Unit and explained what happened. I can only imagine what her conversations with her friends would be like the next day.

I understood the Beatles song "It's been a hard day's night"

****

Some nights were incredibly busy, and I would go home to bed hours late, just wanting an undisturbed day's sleep. However, the phone had different ideas. Kicking the body into life after a couple of hours sleep was not easy. Our house was cold, and I shivered as I climbed into my uniform, kept at the ready at the end of the bed.

It was seven o'clock on a Saturday morning and a person in Frankton, Hamilton disturbed a house burglar. The burglar decamped and there was little foot traffic in the area, so the decision was to call Cara and me into action.

The Waikato Region, in winter, frequently has heavy frosts. Frosts have the ability to kill a scent reasonably quickly and this was a particularly frosty morning.

Frankton was an old railway suburb of Hamilton and was one of the lower socio-economic parts of the city. Old railway houses dominated; three bedrooms and box shaped. The design was to be functional as opposed to attractive.

A man got up to get his early morning paper and milk from the letterbox. He heard a noise in his garage and went to investigate. Bowled over by the offender, who was making a run from the garage, the man picked himself up and ran inside to ring the police.

The Operations room assured me that they had a tight cordon in the area, and no one had left. Technically, such an assurance should have given me heart, but experience showed that cordons might take five minutes or more to set up and an offender could cover over a kilometre in that time.

I was tired and just wanted to go back to my warm bed and was sceptical about our chances of success at this particular job. I now lived in Te Awamutu and it took nearly twenty minutes for me to arrive at the scene after the offender had decamped. It was a fast trip, as I knew the road extremely well and there was minimal traffic to manage. As I neared the scene, I saw the patrol cars cruising slowly around the streets. Even though it was cold, they had their windows down to let the offender hear the radio babble.

I spoke to the complainant, who by now was noticing the cold and was shaking. Fascinated by the arrival of a Police Dog, complainants are uncertain as to whether they should try to pat the dog or not. This one looked at my gumboots. It took too long to put on the regulation boots and lace them correctly.

"Time was precious, so I wore my gumboots. Please don't touch the dog, she is here to work."

I put Cara in her leather harness and caste. She picked up the track. I remembered that falling frost kills a scent, not frost per se. The conditions and time delay made for slow tracking, as Cara had to work hard to keep on the track. The height of her head indicated how fresh the scent was and the amount of hard work involved. On the track, she was snow ploughing the frost to one side. On a still morning, I heard her nostrils sucking in more scent, but I was at the other end of the dog with a different view to her face.

We left the complainant's property and crossed a fence into the neighbours. The pace was slow. A straight line though another three properties and then she deviated towards a shed. Was he trying for another burglary? No. We tracked past the shed and down to the road. Cara's tail was wagging – at least she was not feeling the cold. I noticed the bush by the front gate where his footmarks were. He obviously hid there for a time. This would be when the patrol car first arrived in the area.

The track continued back down the other side of the house before crossing another fence. We scooted across another couple of properties gathering more speed. Since the bush, Cara had raised her head suggesting we were gaining time.

We went around the back of a garage and then Cara sped up with her head rising. Her tail was wagging faster now. The offender had stayed still at the back of a garage for a time before moving on and the track was getting stronger.

The patrol cars radio me wanting an update and I advised the direction we are heading. Moreover, I suspected we were close to our offender. I asked them to tighten the cordon.

We crossed another couple of properties and then Cara went towards the back door of a house. The house had a small veranda, with a corrugated iron roof and Cara stopped at the bottom of it, jumping in the air and barking. Cara was telling me our offender was on the roof. For the life of me, I couldn't see how anyone could get onto the roof. Cara's barking woke the house occupants who came out. I explained what was happening and asked for a ladder. The young guy in his candy-striped pyjamas ran to the garage to oblige. The excitement of an offender on his roof was so much he wanted to go up and catch the offender himself. I couldn't let him do that. I climbed up onto the roof and there tucked under the eaves to the main roof was the offender. He was shivering probably through a combination of cold and nerves. I ordered him off the roof. At first, he refused, so using negotiation powers I advised I would put Cara onto the roof to talk to him if he preferred. Sense prevailed and he followed me down the ladder. The roof was slippery with the icy frost on it. He had to come down slowly into the waiting arms of his captor.

The patrol cars arrived to make the arrest. This was one of the better bits of being a Dog Handler; someone else did the paperwork. I went to the station for a hot cup of tea before heading home for a day's sleep. Yes Beatles, it had been a hard day's night.

17

Helicopters without doors are draughty

Thump, thump, thump, the unique sound of a military Iroquois helicopter splintered the rural silence. We took a break from our silent journey alongside the stream to scan the Kaimai Ranges silhouetted against a pastel blue sky. The noise had arrived, but the picture was still coming. The sound of the rotors thumping their way through the daytime air penetrated our minds, desperate for a break in concentration. A few moments later, we saw a single Iroquois helicopter heading north along the side of the ranges. The camouflage disturbed by the helicopter movement.

Mick the Sergeant in charge of our Armed Offender Squad grabbed his radio and called base.

"Why don't we call the Army and get a loan of their chopper for a couple of hours," he suggested to the boss.

We were searching farmland just out of Waharoa for an armed and dangerous escaped prisoner from Waikeria Prison. During the night, the prisoner had burgled a farmhouse and taken a firearm. He was known for using firearms and so caution was our theme.

The radio stayed silent. Mick muttered under his breath about talking to brick walls. Mick was a Detective Sergeant, of the old school. He had us all convinced he knew every criminal in the greater Waikato area as well as apprentice criminals. His rugged complexion, with curly brown hair sticking outside his black beret in tufts, combined with his solid build and hard-earned wrinkles made his mid-fifties feel real. Mick turned up at one incident with the flu and could not be bothered with the usual negotiation process because he wanted to go home to bed. So he climbed over the fence we were hiding behind, coughing and sputtering just walked into the house and told the offender he was "a bloody fool" and then handcuffed him, walked out, handed his prisoner over and went home to bed.

Mick was a great Sergeant to work with, as he was very practical. His suggestion of the helicopter made sense to all of us, probably because we had been walking for hours. The helicopter noise was diminishing, as it got further away. Mick scrambled up the stream bank and peered over the top. He quickly slipped back down to us.

"Another barn, over the ridge about fifty yards – Bruce, give Cara a run and let her check this one out for us."

Cara and I crawled up the bank and I peered over the top. It was flat farmland and there was an old unpainted corrugated hay barn about fifty yards away. In between was one seven-stranded barbed wire fence. Cara was to operate from either voice commands or hand signals. This situation called for hand signals. I took her lead off and signalled her to go forward. She trotted over the bank and started to head towards the barn. It was obvious she had identified the barn as the place to search. When she got near the fence, she turned her head to check for the next hand signal and over the fence she leapt. She sped up and went to the barn and inside. We waited. The riflemen were lying on the bank beside me with the guns trained on the barn.

We waited. Eventually Cara came out and started to look around the paddock. Her behaviour showed she'd found no human scent. We all stood up and moved with caution towards the barn. We took turns climbing over the fence and then passing our firearms under the fence. We moved towards the barn and then inside. There was no one.

Thump, thump, thump. The sound was getting closer. We looked north and could just make out a dot getting bigger. Mick answered his radio.

"Yes, we can return to base. We will be there in less than ten minutes."

Mick turned around and says, "Helicopter time boys. They listened for a change."

Our energy levels rose, and we started to jog back to base camp. Cara had never been in a helicopter, so I was unsure what was ahead.

It took us about fifteen minutes to arrive back at base and the helicopter was already there with the engine shut down. Both the side doors were removed and lying in the paddock.

"Bruce, will Cara be okay in the helicopter," asked Detective Inspector Phil.

"Yes," I replied confidently.

Then the young pilot swaggered over to us. He was dressed in army camouflage overalls and his face was that of a pimply teenager. He looked as though he must be no more than seventeen years of age. Slim build, about five foot six inches but with teenage confidence making him the Giant in Jack's story.

"Your dog will behave in the helicopter? There will be no doors on it, and you will have to hold onto her when we do some of our manoeuvres or she will fall out."

I assured she probably had more experience than he did.

"I have not had my lunch yet and I don't want her touching it."

I advised him Police Dogs eat on command and his lunch would be safe.

Squad members Neil and Laurie were to stand on the landing runners, outside the helicopter. Mick, Cara and I were in the central part, directly behind the Pilot and co-Pilot. We all got into position inside and the engines fired into life. With the doors off the noise was deafening. The two pilots were okay because they had headphones on. The helicopter shuddered and kicked as the power built up and instantly we went straight up. A bit of warning would have been nice so I could tell my stomach what was happening. Instead, my stomach stayed on the ground while my body was airborne. Eventually the stomach decided to join the rest of me, but the re-union was not a happy one.

Mick hand signalled the co-Pilot where he wanted us to go. We were well above our first barn, hovering. In seconds the helicopter dropped down, side on to the barn giving time for a quick look before we were back up to the point we started. I think my stomach got the biggest fright. It was still on the down journey when my body was going back up. I was glad there was no mirror because I was positive, I was green.

Within minutes, we checked about five to six barns. After the last one, the pilot decided to stay at fence height and fly directly to the next barn at this altitude. This was exhilarating. Up ahead was a stand of tall gum trees and so I braced myself for us going up and over them. Instead, the pilot waited until the last minute, put the helicopter on its side, and flew through the narrowest of gaps in the trees. The draught from the helicopter broke branches off the trees. The floor in the helicopter was sheet metal and for Cara there was no grip. Luckily, I had her lead wrapped tightly around my hand, because Cara was just swinging in the breeze. Her tail end almost knocked Neil off the runner. Neil then described in colourful language what he thought of pimply faced Army pilots.

Once the helicopter leveled out I got Cara on her feet – I could swear she was smiling. The look was one of "You are green boss, but I love this." I then hand signalled the pilot that if he did another stunt like that Cara might have "Pilot Burger" for lunch. The threat worked and he settled down. We were now searching the area in a more sedate fashion and I started to enjoy the trip. The next barn we dropped down to I leant towards Neil to check inside the building. I felt the lead go tight but thought nothing of it. We rose again and the lead was still tight.

Then I felt a little jab in my ribs. I looked at Mick and he was struggling not to burst out laughing. I was puzzled. Then he pointed at the pilot's lunch box. It was completely empty, and Cara was licking her lips. Mick and I both burst out laughing.

The pilots couldn't hear us over the thump, thump, and thump of the rotor blade.

We checked out a large number of spots without finding our offender and returned to base. Once the engines were off Mick offered our services to put the doors back on so we would not hold up the army any further. We all said our farewells and the helicopter took off to head back to its base in Auckland. Once it was off, Mick and I fell over each other with laughter.

"What's so funny," asked Neil. We told him about the pilot's lunch. Neil went straight over to Cara and gave her a big hug.

"Good on you girl, you put that pimply little squirt in his place."

18

In front of the front line

The higher in an organisation a person was the more distant they were from the front line.

Don, the Night shift Senior Sergeant was a neat guy, but like a number at that rank, he lived in fear of those above him. Hence, he was prone to no-decision disease. Don was in his late forties, a former country Policeman and a cricket fanatic. I was the night shift Dog Handler and it was a quiet night. Having a cuppa with Don and the Night shift Operations staff, I started to tease him about forgetting the realities of the street. It was all in good fun and then the 111 light started to flash. No chatting! The operator needed to concentrate on the call. The second operator was monitoring, and hand signalled for me to get on the road. I challenged Don to come with me for one job.   He ran into his office and got his cap and handcuffs.

Don could not keep up with me as I flew down the stairwell to the basement car park. Cara knew my footsteps, standing up, tail thumping against the side of the dog van. When the boss rushed like this, something exciting was ahead. I gunned the engine and then remembered Don.

He eventually got in.

"You're going to have to be faster than that at a job if we are to catch anyone."

"Shut up and drive."

Operations opened the basement door. The radio cracked the silence.

A domestic dispute at Whatawhata with a well-known family.

Past incidents at this family had led to my colleagues being hospitalised – this family was dangerous. A patrol car was already on the way and dogs the back up.

Flying around Hamilton Lake, in my peripheral vision I could see Don clutching the door handrail. His face was extremely pale in colour. The van cornered smoothly at balanced speed. Down Killarney Road at a decent speed and the radio again cracked the silence.

"Dogs return to central. Armed offender incident - Whitianga."

One second the van was doing about 100kph in one direction and the next it was doing the same in the other. The techniques from the Police Driving School were worth their weight in gold to make us feel safe.

I didn't notice Don was not talking. I called ahead for someone to bring out my regulation firearm as I pulled up out front of the station. When the pistol etc. passed through the window, I realised Don was sitting still.

"Senior, you need to get out. I will be away all night – you can't come."

Don was physically shaking. The young Constable rushed around to the passenger's side and helped a pale Don, who appeared to be going slightly green, alight from the van. I gunned the van straight onto the Bridge Street Bridge. The car coming the other way appeared cautious. Later I found out it was the AOS (Armed Offenders Squad) Inspector responding to the call out. I will not repeat what he said to me the next morning when it was all over; suffice it to say my delicate ears burnt.

Luckily, I had refuelled the vehicle when I went in for my cuppa so I knew I had plenty of fuel for the long haul to Whitianga (normally 2½ hours). I didn't have to conserve fuel for the high-speed trip.

There had been a shooting at the local Whitianga Hotel and only the sole local Policeman dealing with the incident. Knowing I would be the first Police to arrive meant no gentle trip. Two guys, with more alcohol than they could handle came into the bar with their hunting rifles. They started to take pot shots at ornaments and drinks. Public safety and a colleague's life are at risk and the sooner I got there, the better. Policing was often a numbers game.

Cara lay down in the back, coiled into a ball under my window. She could brace herself without bouncing all over the van. It was a self-taught mechanism for keeping herself safe in high-speed situations. The jet-black German Shepherd was hard to spot in the corner when she was like this. The journey was over a variety of roads, but the latter stages were through the hills of the Coromandel Peninsula. Coromandel was an extremely windy, up and down piece of road. Through the hill country, radio reception was intermittent.

As I neared Whitianga I came back into radio contact.

"Dogs, where are you?"

I stopped a short distance up the road from where I received the call. The offenders had left the Hotel and believed to be on my road. I was to take a static checkpoint until the rest of the AOS arrived. Great – time for a leak. Dog and man get more relaxed internal bladders.

While waiting, many possible scenarios role-played in the mind. I didn't role-play for the fun of it – it was all about mental preparation for the variety of scenarios that might unfold. About twenty minutes later the rest of the squad arrived. A report came in that the offenders' car was at the end of a long straight, around the next corner from where I had stopped. No one knew if the offenders were still in the vehicle. The first thing to do was check out the vehicle.

A couple of riflemen snuck along the side of the road to check the straight. It was a beautiful night and if a young man was with a woman, he would have fancied it was the perfect night for romance. A full moon danced its light rays across the roadside flax creating a daylight effect. Perfect for the dangerous operation which lay ahead.

The riflemen were back very quickly and reported the car was on the side of the road at the other end of the straight. The Inspector decided it was too dangerous for the squad to proceed.

I was to use Cara to check out the car. I asked for a covering rifleman and we crept up to the corner. The car was easily visible in the bright full moon, but it was close to 800 metres away. To use Cara I needed hand signals to control her and that required getting considerably closer than we were. There was only one choice. We crawled our way along the road until I got close enough to be able to use Cara with hand signals only. The other dilemma was the rifleman had a radio and he reported to AOS base what was going on. On a still night, the radio noise travelled for miles. We calculated how drunk we thought the offenders probably were. They were in a closed vehicle (we hoped) and behind closed car doors. The rifleman came about half the distance and then Cara and I were on our own.

To survive in these moments, I blocked out all risks and relied on sharp wits and instinct. Darkness, my friend, was absent, a silent still night for noise travel, my enemy.

I took the lead off Cara and tied it around myself. I could not afford the risk of the chain hitting the road or her giving problems getting it off when we got close. Cara loved armed incidents. The adrenaline tension in our demeanour kept her extra alert. Her performance was always top notch but on an armed incident, it raised a few notches.

The crawl was a command Cara knew, but it bored her if it took too long to get anywhere. This night was to test her patience and obedience to new levels. Eight hundred metres in daylight, under normal circumstances, was not very far. A rifle bullet travels reasonably fast and for long distances, so all the risky scenarios make it a painful, slow journey to get close to the vehicle. The mind and body were on high alert. Cara was twitchy. She wasn't keen on crawling and I couldn't afford to use voice commands to make her behave. After about 10 metres with me stopping every couple to force her back to the crawl position, she settled down. The motion was like seals on land heading for the water to traverse the distance.

The whole time I was trying to calculate how close I could get to the vehicle. Once near the vehicle I sent Cara forward to indicate if there was someone inside. My problem was the only command I have for such a situation was "find and speak." Translated into human that means she was supposed to bark if she smelled humans. When Cara got close to the car, I realised I was too far away to control the situation. I stopped her and seal crawled towards her. This must be close enough. This did not feel good. The adrenaline was fair pumping. My mind could not afford to race, but there were so many possible scenarios ahead. Coolness wins the day or in this case the night.

Cara went forward. She half crawled, half ran up to the car. She sprung to her feet and was about to bark when I gave her the "drop" signal. The split second it took her to register what was going on felt like half an hour. She dropped by the vehicle. No barking! Huge sigh of relief!

I signalled her to come to me. She just up and runs. I forgot to tell her to crawl. I signalled the rifleman to come up to us. We waited. We waited and he arrived. The radio turned off.

I whispered in his ears; sorry this was not a love scene. We decided to crawl to the vehicle ourselves; he would take the left side and me the right. From Cara's reaction, I am sure the person(s) were in the back seat. An eternity later, we arrived at the vehicle. Looking towards each other under the vehicle we signalled one two three. In other words, on three we leapt into action. Cara, still off her lead was beside me, even keeping her tail still at this critical time.

Three! I leapt up, pistol in hand and wrenched open the back-right door. In pure reflex reaction my pistol drove into his right nostril, while I explained the weakness of his parenting and anatomy. Between his legs was the loaded rifle, safety off.

Cara came alive, barking her head off madly. I yanked the rifle from between his legs and placed it onto the road. The offender, with pistol still assisting nostril breathing, removed from the car. I pulled the pistol back and told him to lay face first on the ground. Cara must not bite, but she was enjoying herself rearranging his clothes without a mark on his flesh. Handcuffs were applied. The rifleman used the same technique, minus dog. He called up for the rest of the squad.

Six hours after leaving Hamilton I arrived back to pack up for the night. I heard Senior Sergeant Don had gone home sick. He lasted until the Whitianga apprehension of the offenders and then told one of the Sergeants to take over from him. He left muttering something about he would never travel with that nutter "Howat" again.

It was a pleasant autumn night and the shift was quiet

Lake Domain Drive has a huge park alongside of it and I decided to take Cara and do some obedience training. The National Police Dog trials were not far away and this year I wanted to win.

I parked the Police Dog van in one of the parking areas and got Cara out of the back of the van. She had such a bond with me that she knew we were going to be doing obedience training. I am calm and the Lake Domain Drive was an area we regularly did obedience training while on night shift. Cara had a run around for a few minutes. I loved watching her jet-black tail bouncing around in a Basil brush fashion. The pint-sized jet-black German Shepherd bitch nearly didn't graduate because of her being so small. I smiled to myself as I remembered how she 'd proved all her critics wrong by being a successful street dog.

We started our training doing some heelwork without the lead. Cara was bouncing, a sure indication she was enjoying the experience. Then I heard what sounded like a rifle shot. My automatic reaction was to look at Cara. If a car backfires she takes no notice, but a gun going off makes her flick her head in the exact direction of the shot. Cara was looking across Hamilton Lake towards the city. This was conclusive evidence to me that I had heard a rifle shot.

"Come quick," I yelled at Cara and started to run towards the dog van. She sensed the seriousness of what was happening and ran ahead and jumped into the back. She was waiting in her kennel when I arrived and closed her in. I jumped into the driver's seat and had not quite closed my door when I heard a second shot. I grabbed for the radio, but too late.

"Dogs return to station – Armed Offenders call out. Don't go through Pembroke Street. All Units please be on standby and keep out of Pembroke Street."

Pembroke Street was the direction Cara had been looking with the firing of the first shot. It was also the quickest route to the Police Station. Pembroke Street was near Waikato Hospital and nearly all the houses were owned by Doctors. It was normally a sophisticated street.

I fired the engine and took off using an alternative route to the station. I had to go back to get my issue firearm. The Operations room dispatched a Constable to the basement with a .38 pistol and ammunition. I drove in one entrance, slowed down with my window open, received the pistol and ammunition, then drove out the other end.

"Dogs take up position at the corner of Angelsea and Pembroke Streets."

I knew the drill well. Most of the armed incidents Cara and I attended we were first on the scene. Our job was to sit still, watch and listen until the rest of the squad arrived. A full briefing would occur when the others assembled.

I turned the radio down as low as possible, so it was almost impossible for me to hear. Now the waiting began. A while later the Detective Inspector in Charge arrived. Phil was slightly taller and similar build to me. We all had huge respect for Phil and at a personal level I had more reason than most. Phil was coaching me to take my Sergeant exams.

"The shots came from a house further along the street on our left. The house was well known – we were planning to do drug warrants on it next week – major dealers."

Phil respected us Dog Handlers and always treated us as if we were one of his Detectives. Others treated us as if we were low life. Within minutes the rest of the squad arrived, and we got into two sections: one at the front of the house and one at the rear. I was with the section covering the front of the house. Mick was the Sergeant in charge of our section; a big strapping male who was one of the most practical Sergeants in the station.

"Let's just walk along the footpath until we are opposite the house and then we'll hide in the neighbouring property," said Mick. As Mick was getting older, he was less inclined to want to climb over fences anymore so he took the most comfortable route.

Cara was on her lead and we nonchalantly walked along the footpath at the rear of the section until Mick hand signalled for us to hide in the bushes directly opposite the house where the shots came from.

Once in position the negotiations start. We could hear the phone ringing in the house and knew that it was Phil trying to make contact. The phone just kept ringing, and no one answered it.

"Operations, have you still got the complainant on the phone," inquired Phil on the radio.

"Affirmative."

"Can they confirm no one has left the house since the shots were fired?"

"Affirmative – no one has left."

In an ideal world, I expected Phil to order the use of tear gas, but there were too many houses and the gas would spread.

"You guys cover me," said Mick.

Mick got up and walking as though on a Sunday stroll crossed the road and went up the driveway. He picked a stone out of the rockery and threw it against the side of the house. No reaction. Mick then signalled us to cross the road and join him.

Mick instructed one of the sections to smash in the door and then throw in the dog. Cara was on full alert. She knew we had a serious situation and she must do her bit. We went up to the door and one of our team kicked it in.

"Find and speak," I told Cara. She was to run in, search the house, and bark when she found anyone. Cara ran in through the door and disappeared from sight. I listened to her paws pattering their way through the house. Then there was silence. She had stopped searching, but she wasn't barking. Mick looked at me.

"What the hell does the silence mean?" he quizzed me. I was perplexed, as I couldn't understand Cara's reaction.

"Let's go," said Mick and we edged our way cautiously into the house. Next thing Cara was back with us. This was the only time I couldn't read or understand the reaction from my dog. We crept along the hallway and the room on the right looks like it was the lounge. Mick hand signaled us what to do. Cara was back on her lead and the rifleman stormed the lounge.

"Oh my God!"

I rushed in behind Mick. In the armchair in front of us was a male in his mid-twenties with a rifle between his knees. He has a calm and serene look on his face. His face was not the problem; it was the wall behind him; his brains splattered across the lounge wall.

"I guess his dealing days are over," said Mick in his casual fashion.

It was impossible to get used to sights such as this one in

front of us. Phil came in with the other squad members and then told us all to get out. The public didn't understand these things; we knew behind lace curtains, eyes and ears monitored our every move.

We all stood around in the back yard and then we started to make jokes, to cope with the shock. Phil came out and ordered us back to the station.

"The neighbours will hear you buggers," he counselled us.

We went back to the station and had a cup of tea. In the kitchen, there were no civilians and we could unwind in safety.

19

Under the cover of a blackberry thorn

The busiest time of the month in Policing was around the full moon. Full moon was the time when you got unpredictable behaviours.

As Police Dog Handlers we worked with the Armed Offenders Squad (AOS) and when they had a call out, it required two dogs to attend. Based in Hamilton, at this time, there were only two Dog Handlers: Fred and myself.

The situation was in a small rural community near Morrinsville. The offender had escaped from Tokanui Psychiatric Hospital and returned to his family home. He was drunk, raving with his hunting rifle and threatening his parents. He was in hospital after committing violent crimes. I attended his escape with Cara, with no luck.

I was low on fuel, so I called into the station to refuel and collect firearms. The Senior Sergeant on the squad decided he would travel with me. Graeme was a stickler for the book and an award winner for indecisiveness. He wanted the flashing lights on but no speeding. It was all very well for him; it was not his family held at gunpoint.

The base where squad members gathered was further away from the scene than usual. The area was flat farmland and there was a full moon. In rural areas at night, radio noise travels for miles. Phil was the Detective Inspector (DI) in charge of the squad. Phil divided the team into two squads. One led by the Senior Sergeant and other by one of the Sergeants. I got the short straw and was with the Senior.

It was not often we got 100% turn out. The reason being if a squad member was off duty and been drinking, they were not safe to handle a gun. This night we were very short staffed. Our squad consisted of the Senior, Neil as rifleman and myself. Our role was to cover the front of the house. Fred and the rest of the squad were to cover the back. Once the house was surrounded, normal procedures would kick in. We would try to make phone contact with the offender and talk him out.

Conversation was kept to a minimum and then we only whispered. Senior was the radioman for our squad, as Neil needed to be free with his rifle, a dog and firearm more than enough to occupy me. Using military tactics, we walked silently towards the house. Neil and I walked side by side with the Senior just a step behind us. The first thing to do was to reconnoiter for a safe spot. The house was a typical 1950's farm bungalow. The house had a reasonable size veranda, corrugated iron roof, nothing fancy, just a plain functional house. Out front of the house was a large uncluttered lawn with a short driveway onto the road. The fence was a standard number eight wire fence, typical of rural New Zealand. There were no trees, shrubs or any other sort of cover for us to hide behind. Across the road was a bit of a mound, dropping into an empty drain. Thin blackberry grew across the top of the low embankment. What this all adds up to was no cover for us.

The three of us held whispered conversations as to what was the safest spot. In the end, the decision was we were best to lie over the embankment with our feet dangling in the drain. Not ideal but it only gave the offender a head shot.

The reality was most people are not as good a shot as they might think and at an incident like this with a drunk with psychiatric problems, he probably couldn't hit a barn wall ten feet away. Well, that was our logic.

We crawled the last fifty feet and got into position. The house lights were on, but the heavy-duty curtains meant we couldn't tell where anyone was located. The good thing was there had been no shots fired since any of us arrived at the scene, suggesting things might have settled down in the house.

Senior radioed into base and asked them to turn the volume of their radio down as it could be heard from our position. The radio noise was the other squad saying they were in position at the back of the house and also concerned about the lack of cover.

Neil and I joked our cover was a blackberry thorn, so if all hell broke loose at least we couldn't be seen. Now the long wait. In some of these situations, you could lie there for hours while all the negotiations occur. Lying on a bank on a cold night, not allowed to move or talk, the next best thing to do was breathing exercises to keep calm. The breathing exercises also helped improve the accuracy of a shot, when required.

The only thing you hear at night was the gentle mooing of a cow or sometimes a local boy racer, racing his car. This night, it was the latter. At least this was a distraction listening to this clown racing his car and then the penny dropped. The car was racing towards the scene. The yelling and screaming from base easily heard. Then silence. Next, we heard voices surfing across the airwaves of the paddocks. Then silence again.

"Squad one. A mate of the offender has just arrived. He wants to talk his friend into giving himself up but this guy was pissed. He has just run off across the paddocks and we couldn't stop him. Keep an eye out as he'll be coming in behind you."

Brilliant. Just what was needed, a drunk village idiot!

The Senior made one of his rare decisions.

"Neil, take that guy out when he arrives."

Both Neil and I started to watch behind us. Next thing we heard the house door bang shut. Our offender had chosen this exact moment to come out of the house. His mate in the paddock saw him and called out. The offender discharged the gun but not in our direction. Suddenly there was swearing on the radio – the bullet had just missed one of the back-squad members. It was a random shot, he wasn't aiming at anyone just discharging his gun.

Cara was animated by gunshots. She wanted to take him out, but the timing wasn't right to release her.

"Fuck!"

The mate was in the drain directly behind us and Neil spotted him. Neil dropped into the drain and with all his force drove the rifle butt into the guy's head. The mate did not go down completely, instead he came up fighting. The two of them were swearing at each other. The offender realised something was happening at the drain and started striding towards us. I slipped the lead off Cara and put her in a strangled hold so she was ready for a fast release. Neil could deal with the guy in the drain as he was unarmed. As the offender started to cross the road, I asked permission to let Cara go and take out the offender. The Senior carefully chose this moment to be in his usual "no decision" state. The offender was crossing the road and was only feet in front of us. To hell with orders, I was going to release Cara. The problem was a technical one. The mate in the drain overpowered Neil and came up the bank. The only thing he could find to pull himself up were my feet dangling in the drain. Suddenly I was sliding back down into the drain and Cara with me.

Neil came back at the mate with punches flying. Cara, who was now loose, decided to take out the mate. I looked up from the bottom of the drain where I ended and there was our offender lowering his gun at Neil. The Senior jumped up and grabbed him. The gun went off, missing Neil by millimetres and into the opposite side of the bank. The Senior and offender were struggling, and my money was not on the Senior. Then screams!

"Drop the gun or I'll shoot!"

The squad from the rear came forward and overpowered the offender. Cara and Neil were sorting the mate out. I pulled my handcuffs out and between us we cuffed the mate. It was all over.

Back at Hamilton Station, the boss Phil opened the Police Club. He put a bottle of rum in front of Neil and me and instructed us we were not to go home until it was empty.

Drivers were assigned to stop us drink driving. Political correctness did not exist and Phil knew how to unwind us.

20

The quest for perfection was a continuous bumpy journey

Climbing a mountain is a journey of one step at a time and training was similar. In the Police Armed Offenders Squad, hundreds of hours of training occur so when a life-threatening incident arises, the training increases the chances of success.

National Headquarters based in Wellington decided that all the Armed Offenders squads were to gather at Hopahopa Military Camp for a weeklong training. Hopahopa was a few kilometres north of Ngaruawahia Township. The military camp was for logistic reasons and they had a strong working relationship with the Police. The huge warehouses were excellent for training the Police Dogs.

The barracks and other buildings date back to World War II. The camp was set on flat ground surrounded by a range of hills. The Army had their specialist SAS group at the camp with us and we had joint exercises. The exercises would only work if we treated them as a real incident.

There was a deserted dairy factory a few kilometres east of the base. A hostage situation was taking place at the factory. Different locations had different squads. Cara and I were with a squad on the outer cordon periphery. There were four other squad members beside Cara and me. All decked out in full Armed Offenders regalia, we took up our position.

Our squad was near a minor intersection. It was a Y shaped intersection with bush at every road face. I parked the dog van on the road ready for a roadblock, if required. It was very boring just sitting on the side of the road, with nothing happening. After a few hours with no cars coming through, we'd all used up our quota of old jokes to amuse ourselves. We joked amongst ourselves for forgetting to bring a pack of cards. A lot of Police work was tedious, and we played cards to kill the boredom.

The area was quiet so we would not upset the public. The radio was silent. We assumed there was action at the dairy factory, but we had no way of knowing what was happening.

"Base to all northern squads. There was a report of a stolen vehicle with fellow terrorists in the area. Please be on stand-by and advise of any sightings."

Base gave us a description of the car and it was obviously a plain Police car. Our ears, trained to the unique sound of a Police car engine, were on alert. A general discussion broke out as to what to do if the car came our way. The Sergeant decided to position the dog van at angles to the road, blocking it so no car could get past. I parked the vehicle across the road with flashing lights going.

I sneaked back to my position as we all hid in the bushes at the side of the road. The waiting game began. This was different to a real situation in that there was no real tension.

The biggest risk for us was looking like fools.

The Sergeant was lying to my right and Cara was in the down position on my left. Everything about Cara's body language suggested she knew we were playing games. In a real situation, she picked up my tension with her ears pricked, listening for anything unusual. This time she was relaxed and looked ready for a game.

"I hear it coming," said the Sergeant. The dog van was in perfect position. They would have to stop their car directly in front of us. We would then negotiate for them to give themselves up.

Around the corner rolled the plain Police car. They were not rushing. We could see four males in the car. I then registered what one of their tactics might be and I gave Cara a little flick on her ear. She hated it and bristled. The "stolen car" stopped and they all stayed in the car.

"Police come out with your hands in the air," yelled the Sergeant.

Then what I suspected happened. All four doors of the car flew open and all the offenders ran in different directions. I didn't hesitate.

"Rouse" was Cara's command. She exploded out of the undergrowth and put chase to the nearest offender. The offender was a Hamilton Detective that I knew well. He was wearing old army overalls as his disguise. He turned and looked over his shoulder and realised Cara was after him. The colour drained from his face and his eyeballs were now the size of saucers. He stopped and with trembling voice said, "I give up."

Cara continued. Our squad was making a huge racket with their laughter.

I yelled out. "Handcuff that one and I will put Cara on the rest." By this stage, Cara had reached one extremely nervous Detective. At first, she hesitated until I yelled "Rouse" again. Then she went in and bit him on the leg. A blood curdling scream erupted from his mouth followed by a description of how my parents were not married when I was born.

Two of our squad rushed up and grab the first offender. They had trouble handcuffing him because they couldn't stop laughing. By now, I was almost up to them and I called Cara off. I then set her off after another offender.

"We give up. Howat you bastard call your bloody dog off" yelled one of the meaner offenders. I let Cara go until she was just about to bite him and then commanded her to drop. This game was better than she expected, and she wanted to bite another one. She was in the down position, only just. She was barking, telling me "let me have another one boss." The rest of the squad joined in capturing the last three offenders and then the Sergeant radioed in that we had arrested four suspects. There was silence on the radio.

One of our offenders confessed that Base told them to run in different directions. They knew no one was to discharge their guns so base was puzzled as to how we caught all four.

That night at the canteen there were feelings over what happened. Detective Inspector Phil congratulated me on the initiative. As he told everyone, that was what Cara was to do and she did her job to perfection. The training was excellent for her and I didn't worry that the Detective took months before he would talk to me again.

21

1981

1981. The infamous, controversial Springbok Rugby Tour of New Zealand. Police gave a united image to the public, but behind the scenes, it was not all clear cut.

Months before the tour, we trained in the use of riot shields, helmets and the new PR 24 long baton. These were strange things for those of us who had been in the job for a while. I had been in many a dangerous situation, but this felt like overkill. My feelings towards the tour swayed. At times I was pro it and other times anti. My anti feelings were different to others I knew. All I could see was our nation divided.

I was on night shift the week of the Hamilton (Waikato) game. My logic was I would sleep until after lunch and then watch everything on the TV. On the Monday night, I arrived at work as usual and got to the night shift line up. My instructions were to be at Rugby Park all night, every night on 12-hour shifts guarding the ground for the entire week. I protested. However, orders were orders. There were to be four of us guarding the grounds. The referee rooms were our base.

I drove up to Rugby Park and parked the dog van beside the referee room.

I got Cara out of the van, put on her lead and did our first formal circuit of the grounds. This was boring. I went back to the van and got Cara's training dumbbell for us to have some playtime. Cara thought this was lovely fun, her tail wagging at 100mph. In her mind, this was the best holiday ever. I had a different perspective, very boring and we were only 30 minutes into our shift. Jim, one of the others, asked if he could join us as we wandered around. He was a neat guy and I always enjoyed his company.

Two nights later, I heard on the radio about a burglary in one of our rural communities and asked permission to attend. Refused! This drove a driven Dog Handler nuts.

Friday night arrived and the same rituals. The bosses warned us to be on high alert as they believed the protest movement was going to do something tonight - if only.

Guess what - same old boring night.

We finished our shift at 7a.m. but had to wait for the day shift before we could leave the grounds. 8am and no sign of the next shift; 9a.m. and I had had enough. As the most senior constable, I decided to call up Operations and find out when our relief was coming, I wanted some sleep before the game. We were to return to the station for a briefing.

The guys got in their patrol car and Cara and I into the dog van, obeying orders, returning to the station. The Duty Inspector greeted us, telling us to get a "little" sleep, clean gears and report by 12 noon. I lived in Te Awamutu so there would be no time for sleep. Poor Jim lived out in the country, so I offered to run him home and pick him up on the way back, which we did, still with no sleep.

When we got back to the station, we couldn't find anyone who knew what we were supposed to be doing. We eventually found an officer with stuff on his shoulder, didn't know him at all, and he told us to get our white helmets and report up at Rugby Park. I asked about Cara and was told I was the Dog Handler, make my own decision. I decided Cara could stay in the station kennels.

Jim and I drove to the grounds, muttering about how hungry and tired we were. We parked in the designated car park and couldn't find any Officer to tell us what to do. Jim and I talked about what we'd been briefed in months before as to what the protestors were going to do and decided we would stand at the top of the open stand, opposite the grandstand, in a position where we could watch the protestor action. We knew there was a huge contingent of Police at the ground, so we would keep a low profile and get the best of all worlds.

We got into the position Jim and I agreed was best. The crowds were gathering, and they were obviously supportive of us, by the amount of advice we were getting on how to manhandle the protestors if we could get near them. We decided our best thing to do was just smile at all the comments and say nothing.

Then our radios cackled into life. There was a report about a stolen plane from Taupo flying towards Hamilton that had threatened to crash into the main grandstand if the game went ahead.

The reports were coming through frequently about the

progress of the plane. It was suggested that the Air Force be dispatched and shoot the plane out of the sky. There were only two people in the plane, so the loss of only two lives compared to large numbers if the threat was carried out. It would be legal to take such action. While this was happening, we could hear the noise of the protestors heading towards the ground.

Jim and I were caught between listening to the radio and the tsunami wave of protestors chanting their way along the street. Then our radios cackled with the instruction for the "Red Squad" dispatched to stop the protestors. We had no idea who or what this squad was. There was a moment's silence and then a voice we didn't recognise came on the radio and told our District Commander to rescind the order. The only person we were aware of with such power was the Commissioner and we had no knowledge of him being at the game.

Then the unbelievable happened - our District Commander pulled everyone back. He was usually extremely strict, and it was hard to comprehend what was going on. We saw Police in riot gear withdrawing into the grounds. This was our first time seeing this gear apart from the training months earlier. Jim and I had our old white helmets and traditional short batons plus handcuffs.

The protestors sensed a change in Police tactics and started to run down the road. They headed to the fence about 50 yards away. There were hundreds of them and two of us. The odds were not favourable. Then the protestors tore the fence down. There was a ridge between them and us and we had no idea how they tore down a large fence. The tsunami was coming into the grounds with swell after swell. They just ran over the football fans. There was sporadic fighting breaking out everywhere. There were about a dozen or less Police at the gaping hole doing the best they could. We now had an irate crowd between our colleagues and us. The protestors swarmed onto the grounds. The football crowd were controlled but angry. The loudspeaker system pleaded for calm.

Jim and I were mesmerised. We suddenly realised the radio was talking about the plane again, getting closer to Hamilton. Then the fence was somehow closed - not sure how and we had a large crowd of protestors on the grounds. The crowd in front of us turned, threatening to do us in if we did not do something about the protestors. It was not the first time in my career I was scared, but this was probably the most frightened I had ever been. We were in a no-win situation. Then from under the grandstand came the "Red Squad" decked out in all their riot gear. The threats at us were getting serious and we looked at each other. With synchronicity and without speaking we ran down the aisle, leapt the fence and ran out to the Red Squad.

The Inspector of the squad got a hell of a shock when he found out he had two extras - two with no idea what they were doing. He agreed with my suggestion, it was safer for us to be with them. Another two squads joined us, and we had the protestors surrounded. Now what! I expected they would bring a paddy wagon out and we would lock up the protestors one at a time. This would take us until dark to accomplish. We held our lines and the rugby crowd was getting annoyed. It felt like we were about to become the filling in a very unpleasant sandwich.

Which way should we be facing? Who was friend, who was foe? For the first time in my career, the lines were completely blurred. The debate on the radio was now around calling the game off because of the plane threat.

Then a rumour flew down the file that one of the "big brass" was coming out to negotiate with the protestors. Suddenly the Commissioner walked through our ranks just a couple of feet below me. Now we would see leadership. I stood in stunned silence as the Commissioner grovelled with the head protestor. I felt ashamed. I could hear every word of the negotiation and this was supposed to be our leader of law and order pleading for the protestors to leave the ground. Police were to escort them to "safety." In that moment, I become pro tour. We were letting an unlawful assembly dictate their terms and conditions.

Police work and safety relies on obedience, not unlike the military, there was no choice but to participate in what was happening - the options were non-existent. The loudspeaker came on saying the game was cancelled because of the threat of a plane crashing into the grandstand and greater public safety. The protestors cheered and the rugby crowd booed. If I thought I was scared before, it was nothing compared to this. Under my uniform I was trembling. I didn't know if any one externally could tell I was shaking, but I was shaking.

Then we parted ranks and escorted the protestors off the field. The missiles were not huge in numbers, but they existed. Then the protestors were out of the grounds and we were to stay and reform at the opposite end of the field from where we started.

At this point, the crowd decided to turn on the press box. A different Inspector yelled "They are attacking the press" and he started to head towards to press box until he realised, he was on his own. Without a word spoken, four squads of Police plus two ordinary cops stood still and never moved a muscle. Silently he turned and walked back to stand in front of us all. I don't know how long we stood there and then we were told to return to the Hamilton station and await further orders. Jim and I looked at each other, then in silence walked to the dog van. We never said a word as we drove back to the station. I couldn't park by the kennels - I didn't want Cara to see me like this.

We went up to the Police club awaiting further instructions. It was about 7p.m. that some officer came in to brief us on the events of the day. I wasn't interested. I wanted to go home, have some food that I hadn't had since that morning and fall asleep. Then this officer asked for the Hamilton staff who had worked nightshift the night before. We quickly identified ourselves believing we would go home. To our shock we were told we were to go straight back to Rugby Park and guard it through the night. I dare not repeat the thoughts that were in my head at this ridiculous order.

Jim and I went down and got Cara who was beside herself. She was busting for a toilet run and food. We both could agree on the latter. I took her down by the Waikato River and gave her a toilet run. Then we loaded up and went to a decimated Rugby Park. I had her bowl and fed her. She was bubbly but read that the boss was not in the best of moods.

I decided I had better be obedient and with Jim we did a circuit of the ground. We said nothing about the day. Cara was tearing around the ground overflowing with energy. She'd slept all day, now fed and watered. I was the complete opposite. None of the hierarchy comprehended we were tired and starving. We'd worked over 24 hours, only eaten twice, and had next to nothing to drink.

I had had enough. I told Jim I was going to sleep in the referee room. Since I was the most senior of us the others decided if anyone was going to get in trouble it would be me. We went into the clubrooms and I lay down on the floor. I had Cara on her lead and told her to lie beside me. Before I knew it, I was sound asleep.

I woke up to deep-throated growls from Cara. Through blurry eyes I realised an officer was standing over me. I (almost politely) advised the officer that we were sleeping and if he continued to disturb us, Cara would have her own words to say. Discretion won and we woke up in time to finish our formal shift.

22

The aftermath of 1981

The New Zealand civil war of 1981 was losing momentum and the country settled into a new paradigm. In the Police we felt the pressure 1981 bought about – we went from being the friendly "bobby" to villains who carried long batons, shields and riot helmets. Instead of protecting the public, we now had to protect ourselves in unprecedented ways.

Turua was a sleepy little farming community of four hundred families on the Hauraki Plains. There were no new houses; most of the houses built at the end of World War II when returning soldiers were balloted farmland in payment for their time overseas. The local economy was based around dairy farming. The biggest crime events were teenagers with internal screaming skulls fighting their journey into adulthood. Therefore, when the call came for the team policing unit to go to Turua for an out of control 21st birthday party, this symbolised the transformation into a new era.

The Thames constable had gone to the party after reports of fighting breaking out. The party was at the local community hall. A weatherboard, plain building that was one big open space inside except for the large kitchen area at the far end from the main entrance. Pre-1981, this incident was insignificant, as he would have told them all to grow up or else, he would tell their parents, and everything settles down. On this occasion he was attacked with missiles such as beer bottles thrown at him. He retreated with cuts and abrasions, calling for back up. He parked down the road to observe. The battle of Turua commenced.

Operations decided to send Cara and me to assist with crowd control and the night shift Detective to mingle among the crowd. The drive from Hamilton to Turua was ninety kilometres and takes an hour – we take less. We drove in convoy to all arrive at the same time.

The team policing unit consisted of a Sergeant and five constables, all equipped with riot shields, helmets, and long batons. Even within Police circles, we were finding the new wardrobe difficult to come to terms with.

We gathered about one hundred yards from the local hall where the party was located. The air was fresh except for the drifting odour of nearby cow patties. I remembered the scene in "High Noon" where the streets are clear before the inevitable shoot out. Our presence created a stir as the teenage drunks gathered in the street to yell abuse and defiance at our mere presence. There appeared to be a couple of hundred youths who had come from near and far. Potential ugliness shuddered through our visual cortex as the scene unfolded.

The Sergeant decided the tactic was to try and get them all back into the hall and use reason to get them all to drive home sensibly. I went with Cara to the far side of the growing crowd and the team police unit formed a line across the road, batons initially to be in holsters, but carrying shields they moved forward. The Sergeant had his loud hailer instructing them to go back into the party.

Detective Del was trying to mingle with the crowd. Del was a handsome man, with deep blue eyes and blond hair that made all the females envious. He was a fitness fanatic and his body, sculptured to perfection, was noticeable.

Cara was on a double lead, so her choke chain did not work in the normal fashion; instead, it held her for me to fan her against the crowd. My protection against the missiles was a soft forage cap, for as Dog Handlers, we used the dog to look after ourselves. Cara sensing the tension was snapping and barking as much as possible. I was on the constant look and listen out for beer bottle missiles. Once airborne it was only the sound of a bottle whistling through the air that gave indication of exactly where it was.

The drunken young men were in a feeding frenzy with the Police presence. I walked along the middle of the road with Cara in front snapping and snarling herding the cows back into the hall. Traffic was trying to get through, as this was a main highway to Thames. The young locals realised our strategy and dispersed in groups around the back of buildings. The situation was getting out of control and looking uglier and more sinister. Instead of fighting amongst themselves, the fun had turned into a new direction of the Police being opposition. Detective Del was behind me by about twenty yards and was in the middle of the left-hand lane. Ahead of Cara and me was a farm utility that had a cowcatcher on the front, or bull bars as they are sometimes called. There were four young men in the front seat designed for three.

The vehicle was in the middle of the road, with the engine revving. I had no idea what was going on in the driver's mind. Suddenly he released the clutch and the tires spun firing black smoke as they struggled to grip the tar seal road. He gunned straight at Cara and me so I headed as fast as I could to the side of the road. The ute, its rear end wagging, got traction and fired straight over the point where I'd been standing a few moments earlier. I spun around to watch what was to be the next move.

My stomach lurched and I was shocked into inertia. I couldn't estimate the speed of the ute by the time it got to Del, but I watched it hit him with the middle of the cowcatcher. He flew into the air about six to seven feet. He was acrobatically flying through the air. It felt an eternity before his body thumped onto the ground and he lay there with no movement. The ute drove off at speed heading towards Thames. I wanted those guys!

The others could take care of Del, my responsibility was to catch the offending driver. I ran as fast as my lungs allowed back to the dog van and let Cara jump in the front onto the seat beside me. Normal protocols flew out the window – one of our own was down and this was a worst-case scenario. The dog van was about fifty yards away from where I'd been standing. I automatically turned on the flashing lights as I ignited the engine. As I went past Del some of the team police unit were at him. I radioed to Hamilton for an Ambulance, giving the briefest of descriptions of what happened.

The engine of the dog van was screaming as I took it to maximum revolutions in each gear. My mind was already replaying the scene that unfolded a few moments ago and nausea bubbled away in the cauldron pot of my stomach. The road was long straights and the night was still. I saw the taillights ahead as I closed in on the fleeing vehicle.

The Turua Road connected on a sweeping right hand bend with the Auckland/Thames Road. Once the roads join forces it wasn't far to the Kopu single lane bridge. As the fleeing vehicle joined the merging road, I lost sight of the taillights. I was puzzled. There was no logical reason for the taillights to disappear. In a few minutes, I discovered why. The ute had failed to take the corner and had gone straight over the merging roads and crashed into the paddock. As I slid the dog van to a halt, I could see human shapes running across the paddocks.

Stopping, I reached across to Cara and took her lead off. I yanked the handbrake on as I decamped. Cara jumped over my lap and was straight over to the vehicle. She knew and understood her role. For the last five minutes, she had listened to colourful language about my thoughts of our offenders. The boss was in a state – we needed to get these offenders. She sprinted to the abandoned vehicle whose doors were still swinging. She did not lower her nose as this was perfect tracking conditions. In the moonlight, I saw ahead one offender and Cara was in hot pursuit. The good aspect was there were no houses nearby to listen to my language as I command Cara to attack. In textbook fashion, she leapt at him, grabbing his right arm and dropping him onto the paddock. He was yelling and screaming with pain, but my sympathy for him was non-existent. In my mind, Del was dead – no one can survive an incident of this nature. My last replayed image of him showed no movement.

I rushed up and was disappointed to realise when this man dropped into the paddock, he just missed his face landing in a cow patty. I handcuffed him. Then a voice on a Police loud hailer breaks the night air.

"Bring him here Bruce and get the next one." The team policing van was waiting on the side of the road. I called them to came across to us and give me another set of handcuffs. Cara was already off after her next one. I quickly exchanged the offender for another set of handcuffs when I heard screams of pain. Cara had number two. One of the team policing guys came with me and took this one back to the waiting vehicle. Cara never hesitated. She was straight away after number three and it took her only minutes to bring him to ground. They were fine young rural men, under normal circumstances, but a belly full of beer slopping around their insides did not keep them in shape for a good run. Number three gone and we were heading towards the Kopu Bridge.

"I give up," yells this pathetic voice. Unfortunately, my hearing was deficient and when the screams start, it was impossible to understand what he was saying. Once I arrived, I demand to know who the driver was before I called Cara off. He admitted he was the driver.

I asked the team policing unit for an update.

"It looks like Del won't make it," was the reply. I rejected the offer of a lift to the dog van. I preferred the loneliness of the walk back to our van as I tried to come to terms with what happened. Cara knew I was upset and knew her work was outstanding. I sat on the ledge on the dog van and she lay down at my feet. Del was a mate and the reality hurts to the depths of whom and what I am. I knew his wife and little children.

Epilogue

Detective Del survived, only just – his injuries were extensive – nearly every bone in his body smashed as well as extensive internal injuries. His extraordinary fitness level saved his life. His recovery was slow and torturous.

23

A father's pride and joy

The National dog trials were looming, and I was committed to competing at them. We had regional trials four times a year and Nationals annually. The best in each region competed for the National title.

Cara was performing at her best, but at trials, there was no room for error. At the end of our cul-de-sac street was a park that was both cycle stadium and athletics training ground. I often went to the park with Cara, even if it was just for ten minutes – just to make sure the obedience was not only perfect, but also fun.

"Dad, can I bring Meg to the park?" my six-year-old daughter asked. When I started as a Dog Handler, the rules stated, "no other dogs allowed" and so I had to give up my German Short Haired Pointer, Greta. It was hard and easy at the same time. One of the shift Senior Sergeants, Alf was a mad keen duck shooter and his trusty old Labrador had to be put down. I offered him Greta and explained why – he readily accepted.

The rules softened and so when Debra turned five, she got her wish, her own dog, Meg a black Labrador. The two were inseparable.

I said she could come to the park, but she must not interfere with Dad and Cara. She quickly agreed, so off to the park the four of us strolled.

She stayed at one end with Meg, Cara and I at the other end. Totally focused on Cara, I took next to no notice of Debra with Meg. When we finished, I saw Debra and Meg just running around. I called them over and we went home.

The next number of trips to the park, everything was the same. Then one day as we went into the park at the usual time, I saw a small crowd sitting on the stadium seats. I thought nothing of it as the park was popular with the local community. I got to my end of the park and Debra to her end.

A short time later, I heard clapping from the crowd. I looked up and the small crowd was looking at the other end, towards Debra and Meg. Debra was standing still with Meg beside her – this did not make sense.

I started doing the next exercise with Cara and the clapping happened again. I looked firstly at the crowd and then Debra. Same result – Debra was just standing there watching me.

This process repeated itself about three to four more times. It got too much for me. I wandered over to the small gathering and asked them what they were clapping at.

"Are you not aware what was happening when you do your work with Cara?" one of them asks. I was perplexed. What were these people talking about?

"When you do your stuff with Cara, your daughter does exactly same with her dog."

I was stunned, especially when they told me Meg was almost as good as Cara. I went over to Debra who was playing with Meg and told her what the people on the bank said. She just smiled.

I suggested we do obedience with our dogs' side by side. Debra readily agreed.

We started with the heel position and walked down the park. Debra had exactly the right amount of slack lead between her and Meg. Meg was bouncing along, with her head looking up at Debra. Cara was doing the same, but she had been trained to react like this. We then started doing turns, about turns, right, left, etc. and Meg was like glue to Debra's left leg. At exactly the same time as I patted Cara and praise her, Debra did the same with Meg.

I then did the down, stay and walk away, Debra copied with Meg. Everything I did with Cara Debra did with Meg. This six-year-old had her twelve-month-old dog doing obedience to the same standard as my experienced Police Dog.

How do I describe the pride I had in my daughter? Through her own initiative she watched Dad, worked out what he did, and copied it with her dog to get exactly the same result. My internal glowing systems were in overdrive.

24

Close to home

A night off and no dog van for any call out. A rare treat – and now a chance to catch up with the family. Our daughters were in bed and I was organising myself for the same ritual – sleep glorious sleep. Police Dog Handlers suffer sleep deprivation as a way of life. We made the most of rare opportunities to try and catch up on sleep, if such a thing as catching up was possible.

I headed out the back door to give Cara a toilet run so she could have a comfortable night. As I stepped off the back steps, the phone in the kitchen rang. There was only one reason the phone rings at this hour – a call out.

On autopilot I rushed back in and answered it. It was John from the local Te Awamutu Police Station.

"Bruce, I know you are on a night off, but Fred was flat out in Hamilton and we have a reported prowler sighted at XXX Street."

The road I lived in ran off this street, and so the "crime scene" was less than five minutes' walk from my Police house. Our neighbour was a prolific prowler and must be a hot suspect. When I moved in, I went across, telling him that he now had a Police Dog living next door, so he had better behave himself. There have been no prowlers in the area since we arrived.

"John, you had better pick me up in the patrol car, just to cover our butts legally if we end up next door."

A couple of moments later John pulled up in our driveway in the white Holden Commodore Police car and we put Cara in the boot. Cara could not believe her luck; she thought she was to have toilets and instead she was back at her passion, work.

In less than a minute, we pulled up outside the complainant's house. John came with Cara and me to the door and the complainant, a young woman in her pink cotton nightie, explained how she was going to bed, went to pull the curtains closed and saw a man looking in at her. I was interested in which window she saw him.

I was fully aware of the legal implications of this job, doing everything to the letter of the law. I put Cara in her harness, casting around outside the window. Cara did her usual high-speed thing where her nose stopped on the scent and the rest of the body failed to stop. After years of working with her, it still bought a smile to my face when she did her start of track ritual.

She had her head reasonably high, which did not surprise me knowing how fresh the track was and in rural New Zealand, foot traffic was not heavy, making for an easier job. She shot from the front of the house, on the street side, to the back – this direction made sense, our offender was heading for the cover of darkness.

We cut across a fence, through another property and then out onto our street. Cara was full concentration, racing down on the opposite side to our house. When we were opposite our neighbour's house, she did a sharp left turn and straight across the road and up their driveway. Down the side of the house she flew, around to the back door that was ajar, head butting it open. She was still tracking, down the hallway and into a bedroom, and then yelps. Her 30 feet of tracking line gave her time to do a brief interview before I arrived. There was our offender, fully dressed in his sneakers. I grabbed him, advised him he was under arrest and cuffed him. I heard voices outside and it was John with another local cop he'd called out.

I handed over the offender and put Cara in the down position. She was showing no signs of recognising her home through the fence. I asked where the car was and John says, "back at the scene." I asked for a ride home and he gave me a quizzical look. I pointed at Cara and then he registered.

He came back a few minutes later with the patrol car, we put Cara in the boot, and all travelled to the station. John then drove Cara and me home. We opened the boot in my driveway and Cara jumped out and trotted off to her kennel. She showed no sign of realising she was just right beside where she'd caught our offender. She was a true professional.

25

Things that go bump in the night

A Waikato winter's night was often foggy and cold, and this night was no exception. As a local, driving in the fog caused me no concern as experience taught me how to be appropriately cautious. The fog drifting in over hilltops and sneaking across farm fences titillates visitors with mystique. Nearly all motor accidents in the fog involved people from out of the district with those from Auckland being the worst. Auckland was the biggest city in New Zealand and was a narrow strip of land with oceans pounding each coastal shoreline. The narrow strip meant winds and infrequent fog.

"Dogs, silent alarm activation at Taupiri Football Club."

"Roger."

The Taupiri Football Club was a very reliable alarm. I had never attended a false alarm at the club and usually it was the same family doing the burglary.

My right foot went harder on the accelerator, but not as fast as my mind. I travelled the back road through farmland and heavy fog. This longer route followed the Waikato River.

This way was windy, but being very close to the river meant less fog. I'd decided to take the river route even though the downside of driving this road meant driving past the prime suspects' house.

"Dogs, which route are you taking?" the night shift Crime Car questioned. The Crime Car was a night shift Detective with a Uniform member as driver. The driver wore civilian clothes and they drive an unmarked vehicle.

The Detective had been grumpy all week. He transferred from Auckland a couple of months earlier and thought Auckland superior to Hamilton. All week I had beaten them to jobs, and he was annoyed at being second.

"River Road."

"We will take the back road, so we cover both routes."

"Roger."

I thought nothing more about it and accepted they might beat me to this job as their route was quicker, but mine was safer.

Cara went into the foetal position in her kennel directly behind me. She stayed curled up until the van slowed at the scene.

Driving alongside the Waikato River on a foggy night was eerie. I drove through patches of fog that force me to slow right down and then into a clearing, accelerating while the vision lasts. Fog teased the trees, not giving away whether it would embrace or avoid. I drove as fast as I felt I safely could.

On arrival at the Football Club I met the usual key holder. He worked at the club and the alarm was connected to the phone at his home. He was dressed in his usual tartan style dressing gown, with sheepskin slippers and old blue corduroy pyjamas. He remembered my last trip when I asked him to make sure he covered his unemployed member as it did not appeal to me. The key holders were on a master file at the Police Station and open up buildings for us. They are not paid; it was part of their civic duty to turn up for the Police.

The key holder was waiting at the driveway entrance to the club; he knew not to go in until the Dog Handler arrived.

"Hi Bob" I called out. He waved me ahead and I flicked my headlights off and drove down to the Clubhouse. Bob would arrive in about five minutes unless I called out for him. The Clubhouse was a two-storey building made of concrete blocks. The roof was a red corrugated iron and the building was functional in design rather than ascetically pleasing. The top floor was where the bar was and where the offenders went to get their free drinks. A kicked in entrance door indicates the modus operandi of the usual suspects.

I got Cara out; she smiled. Another success was about to happen. She'd caught a few burglars here over the years and she went into automatic pilot. The first thing was to check the inside of the building in case one of them was still inside. This worked once when one of the offenders was so drunk, he was asleep on the floor when we arrived.

Cara raced into the building and I heard her paws rushing up the stairs to check out the bar area. I stayed outside and waited for her. She knew what she was doing, and I would hear appropriate sound effects if she found someone. Her feet thumped across the upstairs floor. Within minutes, she was back, and I had her tracking harness at the ready.

Cara pushed her head through the front of the harness and then systematically lifted her front feet, one after the other as her leather tracking harness assembled around her.

"Seek" was her command.

Cara wagged her tail and she spun around the end of the thirty-foot tracking line, sniffing to find the latest human scent. I never failed to be fascinated watching her pick up a track. She cast for the track and as usual, overshot at the beginning. She calmed her body down and settled into her tracking routine. At the start of each track, Cara did a small amount of zig-zagging as she determined the outer parameters of the scent. She was also making sure she was tracking in the right direction. She did know how to back track, which was when we track from an offender and go back over the area they walked, but this was avoided as much as possible to reduce confusion for the dog.

We went around the side of the Clubhouse and headed towards the neighbour's fence. Cara didn't miss a beat as she flew over the fence. I had to keep up as she was attached to me by thirty feet of line and if the line became taut when she was jumping a fence, there was the danger of an unorganised piece of surgery to her tummy.

The houses in the area were all old railway ones with a quarter acre of land. Taupiri wasn't a wealthy area and many of the houses were run down, with old wrecked cars rusting away amongst the long grass. Most looked as though they had not seen new paint in over thirty years. All of this was meaningless to Cara who was concentrating on her tracking role. There was obviously more than one offender demonstrated by the way that she was tracking.

We tracked through a property and then another heading towards the main highway. I knew from experience where we would cross the highway. Just up ahead was a narrow piece and you could sight coming cars with ease. There was also darkness on both sides of the road. Even regular customers as these burglars were, they didn't take "unnecessary" risks of being spotted.

We had just crossed the road when I remembered the Crime Car. They were not at the scene and I had heard no radio contact with them for a while. I decided they were lost in the fog.

Cara tracked through the back of the sections on the other side of the road. The Waikato River was on our right and with each ebb and flow, monitored our movement. Mallard ducks under the willow trees watched us with interest. I carried no torch and Cara being jet black was hard to spot in the night. We also had a reputation for being very silent movers and many an offender had no idea we are after them until too late.

On cue Cara moved to our left and headed towards the usual house. When it was newly painted it was blue, but now there was as much bare timber exposed as paint. We tracked past the wrecked, rusting cars with their supply of lodged water rats. We went onto the little concrete pathway running from the derelict clothesline and to the side door. The door was wide open, and Cara did not hesitate, going into the house and along to the lounge. The door was partially closed, and she head butted the door out of the way.

In the lounge were four very drunk males, sprawled over the floor. Their snoring was rock music at its worst. Cara was keen to interview the first one she found but let sleeping drunks sleep – at least until the Detectives arrived. Talking of which, where were they.

I pulled Cara out of the house, took her harness off, and put her on the lead. She wanted to go back in, but I would not let her. I turned up my portable radio.

"Dogs to Crime Car."

Silence. I waited and waited. I tried again.

"Dogs from Crime, can we meet you at the Football Club?"

"I am at the offender's house. Meet me here."

"Negative Dogs, please came back to the Clubrooms."

I decided something vital must be back at the rooms, because for me to leave the scene destroyed continuity of evidence. If we left and then came back later anyone could claim coming in after I tracked to the house, and there was no way I could dispute what they were saying.

Cara couldn't understand why she was leaving. Look boss the usual routine was you put them in handcuffs and handed them over to a patrol. She just kept looking at me pleading not to leave. Leave we must. I wandered back to the Clubhouse, walking directly through the neighbouring sections until I got to the destination. Bob was there, but no Crime Car. Bob had the outside lights going.

"Bob, where are the Detectives?"

"I haven't seen them Bruce."

I reached for my radio to find out what was going on and I

then heard the distinctive sound of a Police engine. The easily identified unmarked car had a distinct engine noise that tuned Police cars make. Up the driveway came the Crime Car and as it got into the rays of light, I saw extensive damage to the front of the vehicle.

The Detective was driving, which was unusual. As he alighted, I asked him what happened.

"You know the back road well. That big T intersection a few kilometres back – well no one told me there was a bloody T intersection and, in the fog, I didn't see it."

"How much fence did you take out?"

The Detective had got the farmer out of bed and told him he had wrecked the fence, but he would pay for it himself, if no one else knew. The hierarchy frowned upon crashing Police cars and the paperwork was a nightmare.

"You have a panel beating kit in the back of your van, don't you?" He quizzed.

I did but not for a major job like this one. Anyway, the paint can in my van was white; his car was red.

"It will cost me my job," he says. "This was why I got transferred, because I was crashing too many cars."

I smiled a wry smile. It was obvious he was driving too fast; trying to beat me to the job and now he wanted me to fix his mess.

"Let's sort the offenders out first," I said, "then we can deal to your car."

He reluctantly agreed. I sent him and his driver on foot to the address while I did what repair work I could to his vehicle. Bob, once he stopped laughing, gave me a hand.

"How are you going to sort this out, Bruce?" Bob enquired. We had a "pet" panel beater in Hamilton that for a few free beers would do repairs for us. I went into the Clubhouse and gave him a ring.

When we finished shift a few hours later in the morning, the Detective was busy doing the paperwork for arresting four burglars and his car was back in the yard looking better than it had at the start of the night.

Waikato fog was good at hiding surprises!

26

Educating civilians about Police life

Shift work was tough on the body – you never got into real sleep patterns, eating, bowel movements, etc. My brother-in-law (Richard) left school to do a building apprenticeship and all his life worked "normal" hours. He found my sleeping during the day hard to come to terms with. He was a brilliant master artisan as well as a National Brass Bandsman and for those reasons I was extremely proud of him. As an aside, he was a good husband and father, but I don't want to get mushy about that stuff.

His one downside was his acerbic tongue. It always got under my skin when I was on the receiving end about being asleep when I should have been at work. So, I challenged him to come out and spend a night shift with me and see what my world was like.

Technically the rules did not allow Police to take civilians with them, unless they were connected with a crime, i.e. a witness or offender. I figured educating family was very important and therefore it was a work situation.

Richard joined me just after the start of Saturday night shift. The plan was to keep him away from the station so no one would know. I also figured having him out with me on a Saturday night allowed him to recover physically before he started work on Monday.

The dog van was fully fuelled and ready for a night of action. Police Dog Cara was affronted about someone in the front with the boss. She was never sure if someone was out with us whether she was supposed to bite him if he got in the way or leave him alone. She and the boss were the team and a bloody good team at that. The two of us had above average statistics for catching offenders and both took a personal pride in our success.

When there was no action, the expectation was on crime prevention. In other words, driving around usual trouble hot spots and preventing anything from happening. To the un-initiated, it was boring because the average citizen does not have very good powers of observation. Police see anything out of the ordinary.

For two hours, we drove slowly and silently around the streets of Hamilton. The radio made no noise, which was unusual for a Saturday night. Police work was 90% boredom and 10% action, the opposite of television cops.

Finally, the radio beckons us.

"Dogs, prowler XX Naylor Street."

The rest of the detail I picked up as the right foot went hard on the accelerator. Cara responded. She jumped up in her kennel until the first corner, when she lay down in foetal position to brace herself. It was only a couple of kilometres to the scene. An off-duty Policeman believed someone was snooping around his house. Offenders get to know where Police live and are not beyond terrorising family. I had it happen to me when stationed in Lower Hutt.

Although driving fast, no flashing lights were used, as I didn't want any offender to know I was coming. I also made a point of never squealing the tyres through corners. I wanted all the elements of surprise on our side.

Richard received strict instructions to walk just behind me and in line with where I had walked. Cara tracked the freshest human scent other than mine. I could not afford scene contamination. Cara leapt out of the back of the van ready for action. Her impatience at wanting to start work showed as I semi-wrestled with her to put on the tracking harness. With Richard present, I had better do things by the book.

I put Cara in the down position and went to the house to find out what happened. My colleague had had a few too many drinks, which cast doubt on the accuracy of what he was claiming he heard. Casting Cara around where the noise came from, we found nothing. Just my luck – our first job was a fizzer. I put Cara back in the van and hoped this was not how the night was going to pan out. My relationship with Richard would deteriorate if he was left thinking I did nothing all night.

We went back to just driving around the streets. I was not a great conversationalist in the van.

The tone of voice was the first clue something was happening on the radio. I got used to hearing my own call sign above everything else. A lot of time, the radio was full of noise that had no interest to me. Hence when I heard Te Awamutu

Police talking in excited tones I tuned in. Colin had disturbed offenders trying to break into a car at a local car yard on the main road.

I started to wind the engine up and flicked on the flashing lights. I had not been called yet, but Te Awamutu was twenty kilometres away and if any offenders made a run for it, we needed to be as close as possible. Richard had not tuned into the radio so asked what was happening. I explained and told him to hang on because we are about to get our first real job of the night. Sure enough, about five minutes later the call came through for us to attend as some of the offenders had run off into the darkness.

It was a beautiful road between Hamilton and Te Awamutu. The big sweeping banked corners and a four-lane highway allowed for safe speed. I knew the road better than the back of my hand as I lived halfway between the two communities. As soon as I was out of the town outskirts, I got the van up to high speeds. We would get down there in no time.

My brother-in-law was ultra conservative and when he drove, he would rarely get up to the speed limit. He was 100% safe from ever getting a speeding ticket. My mind focusses on role playing possible scenarios ahead and concentrating on the radio talk; I forgot he might be scared about the speed we were travelling. I eased off as we went through Ohaupo Township and then went back up to the old speed. About a kilometre south of Ohaupo, there was the beautiful big sweeping bend and it was a pleasure to drive through it. The problem was a car ahead. It was weaving all over the road and the last thing needed was an accident.

Richard wrote down the registration number for me and after a few scary moments, we got past the vehicle. I called into

Operations and asked them to get a Traffic Cop out to pick this guy up for drunk driving. As I passed, I looked in at him and it was obvious we were from different planets.

A few minutes later, I braked the vehicle as we arrived at the scene. This was a Dog Handler's dream come true. The car sales yard was just out in the country and the night was perfect for tracking conditions. Colin was waiting to brief me. He knew Richard as they went to school together but asked no questions. He showed me where the two offenders ran off into the darkness. He had caught four others on his own but lost the main offender and another.

Blow protocol, this should be quick and easy. I didn't bother to put Cara in her harness but let her "free cast," i.e. without a tracking harness. She ran around the spot Colin identified but would not go past the fence. Richard asked what was happening. I thought the offenders had doubled back once Colin had left to take the others to the station.

Over to the other side of the complex Cara picked up the scent and as quick as lightning she was off. Beside the car yard was a stream with banks covered in blackberry. Cara ran straight down into the stream and raced back up it. I knew the offenders had to be close by her reaction so called on them to give themselves up. They chose not to so Cara received the command to attack. Richard was carrying the torch. I rarely carried it with me, as it was another weighty thing to slow me down.

Then it happened – yelps of pain and yells of call the dog off. I guess this was the early warning signs of my pending deafness as it took me a time to comprehend what was happening. I wasn't going through that blackberry for anyone – it was full of prickles. I called Cara off and told him he had to climb the bank to me. He would not cooperate, so Cara used her persuasive powers to encourage him up the bank. I handcuffed him and muttered about the second offender when he decided to give himself up. He did not want the same treatment as his mate.

I put Cara on her lead and started back towards the Police vehicles with the offenders walking in front of us. Next thing I felt a tug on my jersey. It was Richard. He pointed the torch at the one Cara had caught and there was a big hole in the bum of his trousers and blood. I said nothing. Richard was very white.

Once back at the Police Station the process of dealing with the offenders commenced. I called up Hamilton to check if everything was still quiet, which it was. I decided to help Colin out with all these offenders. I got the one Cara caught and was just about to take him into an interview room when the local Traffic Officer came in with a drunk driver; a member of the Outcast Motorcycle gang. The driver was the one we radioed in about when driving down to Te Awamutu.

I told Richard to come into the interview room with us and sit in the corner. Just as I was about to close the door, one of the Outcast members came to the counter and demanded his mate be set free. He told us there were about twenty of them outside and we were to hand over their mate or else. Colin grabbed him and boot marched him out the door as I stood alongside. The station door slammed shut and was locked.

We all went back to our respective interviews. Whack! Crash! Glass smashing against the station walls! The Outcasts were living true to their name and traditional behaviour.

When a bottle broke against the window frame of Colin's

office, he decided enough was enough. A call to Hamilton revealed they were now busy and there was no back up available. Colin rang all the local off duty Police and then the decision was made we needed to deal with the situation.

Richard was on front door duty. He would let us out and when we came in with a prisoner he'd open the door, let us in and lock it as fast as he could. The plan was to get the biggest one first and then work our way down based on size. Colin was my covering baton man. I went out and grabbed the biggest guy, putting him in a headlock. For some reason he did not consider cooperation. His mates tried to come to his rescue, but Colin fended them off with his baton. On our side sobriety, and a clear-cut objective. On their side, intoxication and no objective. It was exhausting work dragging the gang member backwards, watching all the time for one of the others to get me. Richard was superb on door duty. Once through the door Colin helped by lifting the gang member's feet off the ground and he was carried to the cells. There was no time for recovery as they were in a feeding frenzy outside.

Same tactic and one more into the cells. As we went out for number three, two of the Police Colin called out arrived. Number three was brought back in quickly and easily and then two more Police arrived. It worked! The gang members realised what was going to happen to them and jumped into their cars and all left. Time for a cuppa. There was a huge amount of paperwork before anyone could go home.

I expected Richard to be bored while we processed all the prisoners, but his adrenaline was keeping him pumping.

At 8:30 in the morning we left the Te Awamutu Police Station for me to take Richard home. On the way home, he turned to me.

"How do you concentrate to do all your paperwork after all of that?"

The cuppa was the secret. Years of conditioning meant we knew how to pump up quickly, but equally how to settle down quickly. Richard had a night to never forget and for years afterwards at the family Christmas functions I heard the story again, but not from me.

Hanging by a thread

Phil, the Detective Inspector of the Armed Offenders Squad (AOS) was at night shift parade. When Phil came to the change of shift it meant something big was "going down."

Phil was 6'2" tall, solid build, wavy light brown crew cut hairstyle, and I gathered from what some of the Policewomen said, he was handsome. The phrase a few use – "I wouldn't mind his slippers under my bed."

Phil advised there was to be a dawn raid by the AOS in the Coromandel Peninsula. The Criminal Investigations Branch (CIB) had very reliable information that a dangerous escaped prisoner was hiding in a bush hut in the hills at the back of Tairua. It would not affect the shift, but as the night shift Dog Handler, I had to attend and there would be no dog coverage in the city. The AOS were leaving at 1:00a.m. and I was to report to the squad room at that time.

The escapee has a history of violence and a propensity to use firearms. The property was about a kilometre in from the nearest road, so we had a good bush trek ahead of us. Phil wanted to "hit the house" just on the break of day. The drive was going to take about two hours, before we started the walk in the dark.

The drive to the rendezvous point was routine. We gathered for our next briefing.

Phil allocated staff into the various squads and for the first time ever, Cara and I stayed at the base. The base was right next to the house. Phil wanted Cara to be available if the escapee made a break for it and she could "take him out" with ease.

It was a beautiful starlit night. The bush was dense, dark and the scent of dew on ferns tantalised our sense of smell. There was no clearly defined path and no torches allowed until it was over. The ten of us started the trek in to the cottage. I let Cara run free until we got close. She loved the bush - all new and exciting smells to check out as she darted here and there. The major danger was she gave one of the squad members a fright. Cara was small and jet-black except for three white hairs in the middle of her chest. She was able to move with speed and silence at the same time.

The bush trek was slow as we had no clear path to follow and so we often stopped to debate with hushed voices whether we were heading in the right direction. After about twenty minutes, we saw the silhouette of a tin bush cottage ahead. The lead member signalled everyone to stop. We were too close for voices, for in the silent night even a whispered voice booms.

There was still an hour to go to the break of dawn. The bush wrapped us in the night damp. The thought of another hour was too much. Phil decided we would wait no longer. He signalled the two squads to move into position. One would enter via the back door and the other via the front. Phil and I were watching the front door and squad. We waited for the back squad to have enough time to get into position, and then Phil signalled the front squad. They smashed down the front door and rushed inside yelling, "Police, this is a raid." We heard the back squad making similar noise.

Cara lay on the ground beside me, her expression showing annoyance at not being involved in all the action. We heard the squad members inside the house; they were moving through it checking rooms. Next thing Cara was on her feet and pulling at her lead. She wanted to go into the bush behind the cottage. I held her tightly. One of the squad members called out "House was empty, Sir." Phil stamped his foot in disgust and annoyance.

"Excuse me boss, but I think our offender is in the bush," I advised Phil.

"Impossible," was Phil's retort.

"Check out Cara" I argued as I pursued the matter.

"What are you suggesting," he scoffed.

"Let me let her check out what she was indicating. There can be no harm in that." I offered.

"All right," his voice settled down to consider any possibility.

I took the lead off Cara and she bolted for the bush. I gave her the attack command. If my suspicions were right, we had a very dangerous person in the bush, and I wanted her to get him.

We waited and waited. We could hear Cara in the bush, and she did not appear to be moving away from one spot. I egged her on. I decided to move towards her. Phil ordered a rifleman to go with me. I kept encouraging Cara even though I didn't know what was happening in the bush.

"Rouse, rouse" followed by "good girl."

Then I heard her growling and then a slight scream. I deliberately dropped to the ground and so did the rifleman. Phil also dropped down and ordered another couple of riflemen to come and give me cover. I pulled my regulation Police .38 pistol out of its leather holster and crawled forward, through the next layer of bush, working as silently and fast as I could. Suddenly there was Cara in front of me and she was biting our escapee. He was doing his best not to make any noise. He was in his mid-thirties, unshaven, unkempt hair, with just black and white striped boxer shorts. His white skin contrasts in the moon rays with Cara's black coat.

"Police, put your arms in the air so I can see them."

He put his both hands up and asked ever so politely for me to call Cara off. Two of the riflemen rushed up as I went in, turned him onto his stomach, twisting his arms behind his back, and put the handcuffs on. I checked the riflemen had the guns aimed at him, not me, throughout the whole procedure. Cara was pulling at his legs trying to drag him out into the open. Her black fluffy tail was wagging furiously. She loved this. We helped her. I then called Cara off and put her back on her lead.

The prisoner was taken back into the house and one of the squad members, a Detective, started to interview him. I was standing around talking with Phil and the riflemen and Cara was lying by my feet. The grass was long, at least eight or nine inches. Cara was washing herself, which was usual. By this stage, those with torches were using them to check around the grounds.

"Are you bleeding, Bruce?" one of them asked me.

"No, should I be?" I laughed.

"Well what is all the blood at your feet?" he asked.

I grabbed his torch and looked down at the grass at my feet. There was blood everywhere. I then realised Cara was washing her paw. I made her roll onto her back so I could examine her properly. Her front left paw pad was hanging by a thread of sinew and she was bleeding heavily. The squad had a first aid kit with them, and I grabbed for it, got a bandage out, and wrapped her paw to slow down the bleeding. She needed to see a Vet – fast. My heart was bleeding for my wee girl.

Phil called Hamilton and asked where the nearest emergency Vet was located. We waited for ages and eventually they came back that I would have to take Cara to Thames. I decided our quickest way back to the vehicle was to let her run, knowing it would cause damage, but it would take too long to carry her out. My guts were churning; Cara and I had been through too much together – I just couldn't stand the thought of losing her. I struggled to hold back the tears as we got through the bush as fast as we could. I had always joked with my wife never to ask me to choose between her and the dog – my life relied on Cara.

We eventually got back, and I lifted her into the back. The blood was coming through her bandages and she was not her usual chirpy self. Cara had a huge pain threshold, but this injury was a test. She lay down and I wrapped a couple of my jerseys around her. The road back to Thames was windy and hilly, but I didn't want to go slow – I wanted emergency help as fast as we could get it.

I kept trying to look in her kennel through my rear vision mirror, as we weaved and wound our way through the hills, but she was lying down. Many a time I was tempted to stop and check on her but getting to the Vet quickly made sense. Eventually we came down out of the hills and turned right into Thames. I didn't slow down as we came into the township, but the Vet was on this side of town, so we quickly came to a screeching halt outside the clinic. The trip was normally forty minutes, but we did it in less.

I rushed around the back of the van and opened the door, fearing the worst. Cara was just lying there, and her kennel was blood red. I was sure she was smiling at me as I climbed in and started to lift her out.

"Can I help?" called the woman Vet, in her green overalls. Her voice had a calming effect on me, and I struggled to hold back the tears as I said yes. The Vet was in her mid-forties, about 5'6" and medium build. I wasn't paying much attention as to how attractive she was; I just wanted her to put my Cara back together again. She had an old grey blanket and we put Cara on it and carried her into the clinic. The clinic smelled of disinfectant and a distraught animal odour.

"Are you all right? Should I call a Doctor for you?" asked the Vet. At first, I was puzzled and then realised my uniform was covered in Cara's blood. I almost lost it.

"It's Cara's blood," I explained. She smiled and I relaxed just a bit more.

"Let's put her on the surgery table," she instructed.

"I need her to sit so I can examine her paw properly," she told me. Dragged out of bed to tend to an injured Police Dog and she was caring and sensitive. We both lifted Cara onto the stainless-steel table. The polished top was slippery, but meticulously clean.

I commanded Cara to sit and she obeyed. Next thing the Vet had a bandage and looked like she was going to muzzle Cara.

"What are you doing?" I enquired.

"She's a Police Dog and I am not treating her without a muzzle." I realised the Vet was nervous of Cara.

"She will give less problems not muzzled," I explained. The Vet looked deeply into my eyes to see how trustworthy I was. She started to unwind my poorly administered paw bandage. The pad falls away, swinging on a single thread. Cara received local painkiller and stitches. She sat still through the whole operation, watching the Vet with intense interest. When the Vet finished, she looked into Cara's eyes and Cara gave a big lick as thank you.

****

Cara caught the escapee in the rubbish tip for the cottage and there were broken bottles everywhere.

Cara was off work for three weeks for her paw to heal and so I used the opportunity for one of the rare chances to take some annual leave.

28

My love of flowers

There was a lot of radio activity, but nothing for us. We slowly patrolled the streets, our eyes darting here and there looking for the unexpected. Cara always stood up in the back, watching out her side window. She barked if she saw someone running, otherwise I had no idea what was going through her mind.

The Waikato winter night was fresh, cold and invigorating. As a Dog Handler, the weather played a significant role in how I viewed the night. This night had good conditions for tracking. I knew from experience that when the radio talked constantly something was going to happen for us.

We were driving through Frankton when the call came in about a prowler over near the Claudelands Showgrounds. Cara responded to the surge of power through the van engine and settled into her foetal position behind my window. The objective was to get there as quickly as possible, but also quietly. On still nights, the vehicle could be heard from a distance and I wanted the odds in our favour.

I wanted to talk to the complainant as quickly as possible - time was precious to us if we were to be successful. I found the street address easily. For a change, they had big numbers on their letterbox. I went to the back of the van, flipped open the back door. Cara's tail was thumping against the metal side of her kennel - action. I slid the bolt to her kennel, and she charged to the back and over the tailgate, ready for work. I got her lead and tracking harness and then put her in the "stand" position while I put her lead on. We approached the front door and our complainant appeared; a woman in what I guessed was about her mid-forties, with brown dishevelled hair. She had obviously been asleep, and something had woken her.

I was interested in where the suspect had been, so we had a starting point for our track. The complainant heard a distinctive noise down by her bedroom window and wondered whether it was a potential burglar. I had all the information I needed, as she did not see anyone to give a description. I advised her that a patrol would come later on to get the full details, but now the focus was on trying to locate the offender.

Cara stood still while I took the lead off and put her harness on. She was full of energy and as soon as I released her from between my legs, she sprinted out to the end of the 30-foot tracking line to begin casting around for the scent. Not only was Cara a great tracker, she was fast. She raced across the yard to the back fence and over we went. City fences were so much easier to cross than rural ones.

She was tracking with accuracy and speed. Even on a cool night, it didn't take long for me to break into a sweat. We went through a number of properties. With experience, you know you are gaining on any suspect and it seemed we were.

I radioed into the Operations room giving our location so they could move the patrol cars circling the area. If it was daylight, I would be admiring the well kept gardens we were trampling, but there was no time for sightseeing.

Another fence came up - a nice low wire one. This one would not cause any problems. Cara was over and pulling hard on the tracking line. I was running as fast as I could, so I didn't slow her down. Up I came to the fence and over. Well, somewhat over - my left boot tangled itself in the top wire and instantly I verbally explained to the fence its pedigree. As I cussed I fell. Falling was not unusual, but the stake holding the lovely flowers in place was straight into my right eye. The pain was instant and excruciating. I fell completely to the ground, how far the stake went into my eye I didn't know, but I had never felt pain like this before.

Cara was pulling on the tracking line, but I couldn't continue. I slowly got to my feet, but suddenly felt nauseous. I started to stumble around my eye flooded with water. I knew I couldn't continue. I called into ops and explained what had happened. They offered to send an Ambulance out, but I refused.

Cara was frustrated but sensed that something was wrong. I unharness her and slowly made my way back to the dog van. I then drove myself to the A&E at the Hospital.

Concussion.

NB: About six months later the diagnosis was a damaged eyeball and permanently suffering from double vision. Cara adapted well to be a "guide dog."

29

Tamahaere

Another night of night shift. Most of my time in Hamilton there were only two of us, Fred and I alternated weeks on night shift. We were good mates, but the system meant we didn't catch up often.

Burglar alarms make up a lot of our work; we always treated them as a potential burglary until proven otherwise. Some alarms were extremely reliable, and others operated at the other end of the spectrum. Tamahaere Football Club was a reliable one.

Therefore, when the radio call came in that the club alarm had gone off, I was optimistic of a successful outcome.

The club was surrounded by racehorse paddocks. These differed from others in that they had half round wooden fences with a "hot wire" system across the top half round. The hot wire means electrification to stop the horses getting out. These are pedigree racehorses and worth a lot of money.

The night was calm and there was a reasonably heavy dew on

the ground. Most club burglaries were for alcohol and this one did not disappoint. Cara was getting old; she had hip dysphasia and arthritis. Her jumping skills were not as strong as they used to be.

The two of us arrived at the clubrooms, met the key holder, even with the kicked in door. He knew the routine and stayed in his car until after I had arrived. I got Cara out of the van. Even with her failing health, she loved her work and never flinched at doing her job. Her tail wagging, I put her in the tracking harness and cast her around near the clubroom doors. Her head was down, and I could hear her nostrils working hard, sniffing for the inevitable track. She quickly picked it up and off we headed. No surprises here, the offender(s) were heading quickly for darkness and into the paddocks. This was dumb on their part as the spooked horses made noises that aroused the trainers. We came up to the first fence and up Cara automatically went to jump it. She didn't get the required height and hits the top wire. She let out a blood-curdling yelp, but landed on the ground continuing like the pro she was. I was not so pro. I hated these fences because it was almost impossible for me not to get an electric shock.

We tracked across the paddock and I heard the horses in neighbouring paddocks getting restless with us in their territory. We carried on and came to another fence. Cara was a bit cautious this time and it cost her. She really hit the hot wire and it jolted her in the air. It was horrible to watch my lovely companion going through this, but we were professionals and must push on.

The same dynamics happened at the next fence, but Cara was getting a worse jolt. As she approached the next fence, she just stopped, turned around and looked at me with pleading eyes. Decision time! Do I force my dog on, when the direction we were heading in suggested a vehicle had probably been used, or do I stop? I decided to stop. The Duty Senior Sergeant was angry when I radioed in to say I had stopped tracking.

Cara and I found our way back to the van via gates to stop her getting any more shocks. I decided to call into the Police Station and explain my decision to the Senior Sergeant. Afterwards Cara and I went to one of our training spots and I put her through a series of jumps. At first, she was reluctant, fearing a shock, but quickly realised she wasn't going to get hurt. Understanding, reading and knowing your dog was vital to the success of a good Dog Handler. Later in the night, we made a great catch which would not have happened if I hadn't made an unpopular decision at Tamahaere.

30

An old favourite was back

Police Dog Cara and I went to the Narrows Golf Course club for alarm activation at 3a.m. on Sunday 23rd January. This summer meant hot humid days and sticky nights. It was hard trying to get a good day's rest in this weather and towards the end of the week I was starting to get scratchy through sleep deprivation. My daughters were young (seven & two), making it almost impossible for them to understand the concept of quiet for Daddy to sleep during the day.

Our dog van got very hot in the cabin and I had the windows down to keep air circulating through the van. The activation at this hour was halfway to my home in Te Awamutu, so with a bit of luck the two of us could deal with this job, get home, and get some decent sleep before the sun came up into full strength.

"Dogs from Operations."

"Dogs."

"Keyholder has called in to say there has been a burglary at the club and he disturbed the offenders. They have decamped in a vehicle. You can stand down if you want."

"Anything stolen?"

"Yes, but he thinks they've thrown the property out near the Waikato River."

"Roger. We'll continue and do a property search by the riverbank, since we're so close."

Cara located property with fresh human scent, and these sorts of jobs were the easy ones to improve our statistics. Every time I got Cara out of the van, I had to report it and we strove for success.

We drove down the Narrows Road hill and the Golf club was to our left, a white two-storey weatherboard building. The car park was stones and noisy, a deliberate strategy by the Golf club to reduce burglaries and vandalism on their facilities. The Golf course rolls alongside the mighty Waikato River with massive willow trees weeping into the current. The bank above the river holds a large stand of pine trees woven in intimate cuddles and whispering to one another.

I cruised our dog van into the car park. The Golf club was alight, and the Club Secretary was standing outside the main doors. Like many called out during the night, he was still in his pyjamas and dressing gown. My guess was he was about fifty years of age and probably one of the locals who owned a ten-acre lifestyle block of land. I approached and introduced myself, asking what happened and where did he believe the stolen property had been thrown.

After getting the necessary information, I went back to the dog van to get Cara out and I heard the distinctive sound of a

Police Holden engine. I looked up to see the night shift Detective turning off Narrows Road and into the car park. I waited for Paul and strolled over to chat.

I explained the offenders had left but the key holder saw them throwing stuff near the riverbank where their car was parked. I would use Cara to search the area. Paul wanted to know if it was okay to come over once he'd talked to the key holder. Normally other Police stay in their vehicles until Cara and I have started, as I didn't want them fouling a possible track. This was different; Cara was not looking for a track, but property and she operated under a different command.

Cara knew by lack of urgency that she wasn't tracking, but she was still standing up in her dog van kennel, tail wagging and enthusiastic to work. She was nearing the end of her career, but her passion, energy and drive was still there as she battled her arthritis and hip dysplasia. I opened her kennel door and the first thing she did was wash my face with her big pink tongue. Wal, her replacement, was in the other kennel. He was a young pup but had the traditional German Shepherd colours of tan body with a black saddle image on his back. He was only six months old and was already bigger than Cara. He looked annoyed at the disturbance and just wanted peace and quiet so he could sleep.

I grabbed the lead and Cara knew this meant no tracking. She jumped out the back and headed towards the pine trees. I commanded her to start searching for property and her tail wagged more furiously. She was getting to work. It couldn't get any better than that. I normally didn't carry my torch, but for this job, I took it with me. Under the pine trees, it was extremely dark and so I relied on sound to know where Cara was. She was systematically working from the edge of the road, back towards the golf course itself. She darted in and out of the trees. I marvelled at her sense of smell; the pine needles irritate my nostrils and my sense of smell didn't match hers.

We made good progress and were about halfway between the road and the golf course when the sound of Cara's movement stopped. A moment later, I heard a sickening thud. I flicked my torch around and I couldn't see her. I was unsure of what had happened and where she was. I started calling her to came back and in response, I got a deathly silence. Where could she be? She always responded quickly and efficiently to the "come" command. My torch was going everywhere, and I started to worry.

"What's happening?" queried Paul as he approached.

"I can't find Cara," I responded.

"I said you should have a white dog, we'll never see her in the dark," he teased.

I slowed my torch movement down and then saw part of the bank looked a bit different. I went over to investigate and saw that part of the bank had broken away. I looked over the edge to the darkness down by the river. The Waikato River was the largest and longest in New Zealand and has claimed many lives over the years. I hoped Cara fell into the river as she was a strong swimmer and then I remembered the deathly thud – I had not heard a splash. I got closer to the edge and shone my torch onto the rocks directly below. There was Cara lying still on the rocks, too still. I believed my dog was dead. It was about fifty feet from the top of the cliff to the hard rocks below. Tears welled up within me and I was stunned into silence. Paul came beside me with his torch shining on Cara.

We both just stood there in silence. Cara had caught Paul a dangerous murderer on a past occasion and he was almost as fond of her as I was. Luckily, Paul never turned his torch off from shining on her and then he yelled, "She's breathing!"

My watery eyes stared harder at her and I realised he was right. How could I get down to her? We started moving along the bank to find a reasonably safe spot. Paul knew I was emotional and would do anything to get to my dog. We had been through so much together it couldn't end like this. Paul was the voice of reason. Even if I found a way to get down to her, how could I get her back up? She was seriously injured.

Paul suggested we got the Fire Brigade out with their rescue boat and rescue her from the river. This made total sense. I called on the radio to Hamilton Central and asked them to call out the Fire Brigade, explaining what had happened.

"Dogs from Senior," called the on duty Senior Sergeant.

"Dogs."

"I am not calling the Fire Brigade out to rescue a dog."

I was stunned into a disbelief of silence.

"Dogs to Senior, can you please arrange for a rifle to be sent out and please record it was your decision to destroy an expensive, successful Police Dog."

The radio went silent. Paul and I just looked at each other. We couldn't believe what was happening. We waited for an eternity.

"Dogs, Fire Brigade are on their way."

Both Paul and I went back to the cliff and shone our torches down on Cara. She was still not moving beyond her chest erratically going up and down. The key holder and Paul's driver arrived. None of us knew what to say so the four just waited in silence, no eyes coming off the unconscious Cara below.

About twenty minutes later, we heard the vehicle engine noise of the Fire Rescue Unit. The young driver rushed out to the roadside to guide them in. His face said that finally he could do something useful.

At about the same moment we saw movement from Cara. Not a lot and it was obvious she was in bad condition. Senior Fireman Graham Magner came over to me and I explained what had happened. His crew got a large spotlight out and light up Cara. I think I preferred the darkness. I found seeing her very distressing. Graham and his team explored all possibilities.

"Bruce, we can lower me down to Cara, but I have no idea how to get her back up," said Graham.

I suggested they train me. Graham explained they couldn't legally let me go down on their gear and how would I bring her up. Paul then suggested putting Cara in her tracking harness and tying the harness to the rescuer. The consensus was this was the best approach. To the uneducated, a tracking harness was a confusing looking apparatus. I did my best to explain to Graham how to put her in the harness, but it was hard without a real dog to demonstrate. I remember Wal was in the van, but he had never been in one and was too big for Cara's harness. The harness was set for the individual dog and although I could alter it to fit Wal, I couldn't guarantee getting it back into the right size for Cara.

We all agreed to lower Graham with their winch system and kept the spotlight on Cara. I could talk Graham through putting it on when he was down there. The next concern for Graham was how she would react to him. I promised to keep talking to her to prevent anything happening. Inside I believed she was so injured she was incapable of doing him any harm.

The Fire Rescue Unit moved as close as possible to the cliff and the arm went out with the winch on – Graham was in his harness and lowered over the bank. In a few moments, he was down beside Cara. She tried to stand up, but just fell over. Graham patted her and she licked his hand. He then gently put the front part of the harness over her head. No one made a sound. I suspect most were like me, forgetting to breathe. The river was flowing fast; the silence was still.

Graham now had to lift Cara to get on the rest of the harness. In the light, we saw Cara gazing into his eyes, not like lovers, but as wounded to the rescuer. Now Graham almost lay on top of Cara as he tied his harness to hers. I never realised any of us could go so long without breathing. Then Graham's radio cackled.

"Bring us up very slowly."

The winch slowly revolved.

"Everything is going to be alright," he cooed to Cara.

"Stop," he instructed. The winch made no sound and we all waited in anticipation. The curved nature of the bank meant we had lost sight of Graham and Cara. We saw the winch cable swinging a bit and then, "let's go nice and slow." Then "stop." Again, a lengthy silent wait and "let's go nice and slow."

I then registered I needed to get Cara to a Vet urgently and asked the Operations Room to call out the Vet we used. I would meet her at the clinic in about forty minutes.

Then slowly we saw the top of Graham's helmet and then Cara. Graham has his back to the bank and Cara was on the outside. I rushed over to them and we untied Cara from Graham's harness. I gently lowered Cara to the ground. She looked up at me and those eyes say, "This is not good boss." I asked Paul to help me get Cara to the van and we gently placed her in the kennel.

I went over and thanked Graham. He commented he had a sore back but was more interested in the state of Cara.

"It's serious. I'm rushing her to a Vet now. I'll let you know how it all went. I cannot thank you enough."

I rushed to the van and started the journey into the darkness of the night, before the light of dawn.

****

- Cara was off work for four weeks with a ruptured spleen, lungs and the biggest imaginable black eye. I parted her fur to see the black eye as her fur camouflages it. The other clue to her black eye was one side of her face was noticeably swollen.
- Graham suffered cuts and abrasions through putting himself between the bank and the dog.

- Four weeks after the incident Cara and I went to the Fire Station so she could say her own thank you. She jumped onto the front bumper of one of the engines and then proceeded to lick his face as a thank you to Graham. The local press was present, and their headline read: "An old favourite's back."
- Cara got back to full duties.

31

The phone rang at an inconvenient time

I had just sat down to the family dinner. The phone only rang
for one purpose - a call out.

The Sunday night after seven nights of shift was always
welcome because it meant three days off. At that moment
there were only two Police Dog Handlers in Hamilton, New
Zealand. Fred & I rotated, doing one week on night shift, on
call all the time and hopefully the following week would be
quiet to catch our breath. This particular week was rough with
a couple of very narrow escapes on the job - narrow escapes in
the sense of personal safety being at risk, but that was part of
the adrenaline rush of our work.

After answering the call, it was straight into the bedroom to
throw on a uniform as fast as I could. My daughters loved it
because they could go outside and let Cara out of her kennel.
The girl's toilet ran Cara while I got dressed. Seconds were
precious if Cara and I were to have a chance at catching our
offender. The girls knew Dad would even forget to say
goodbye or goodnight, but they also knew no matter what

hour of the night he came home, he would sneak into their bedroom and give them a gentle fatherly kiss on the forehead.

After the call out, I went to Hamilton Central Police Station.

I was slack at doing my files and never came close to enjoying it, so it was always left until Sunday night to do the week's paperwork. The dog section office was on the first floor of the Police Station. It had a wonderful view from the window, looking down on the roof of the prison block. Whenever I gazed at that roof, I reflected that part of the job was filling that complex with official guests. It was a revolving/revolting door syndrome. I knew in my heart of hearts that the system was an abject failure. Once you put one in there for the first time, I knew they were going to be a regular until they outgrew the silly life. Going to prison became a badge of honour that the average citizen couldn't comprehend.

Reality struck home. The phone rang.

Operations: "Offender on premises in Garden Place" in the central city. The adrenaline automatically kicked in and down the stairs I flew, two to three at a time. It never paid to be in the stairwell during a call out. I remember early in my career rushing out the door of the typing room at Wellington Central and bowling the Commissioner flat. He looked up from the floor and said, "Must be urgent. Don't stand there gawking at me, go and get them."

Into the basement I flew, and Operations had the garage doors open for me. Cara bolted upright and her tail thumped against the kennel walls with excitement. Her replacement, Wal, sat up and like a human teenager muttered about the disturbance.

The job was a fizzer. The offender overheard one of the radios that dogs were on their way. Tattoos were not so fashionable, and I didn't think he fancied ivory scars on his buttocks. I got Cara out at the scene anyway because a small crowd was gathering and her barking at everyone created a funny sense of safety and security for them.

I chatted to the boys for a few minutes and then remembered that dreaded pile of paperwork. I lowered the back gate of the van so Cara wouldn't have to jump so high. A cold foggy, damp Waikato night did not mix well with her arthritis and hip dysplasia. As she slowly got into the vehicle, she regarded young Wal with a look that says, "It was a good, hard life, but I'm glad you are taking over soon." Wal had about six months more training before he would work the streets.

Returning to the station as I drove down Victoria Street, I saw a young white guy, late teens, possibly early twenties, reasonably smoothly dressed for that hour, against the wall of a building. My sixth sense was baseball batting me around the head - this young guy was up to no good. I pulled up alongside of him and saw the pen in his hand. It looked natural - someone who was used to these dangerous weapons. Don't underestimate the power and strength of a well-used pen. Their rabid cuts have inflicted lifelong wounds in many a soul.

On the wall of the building were paper party hats with obscene graffiti written on them. One not so innocent looking young guy armed with a pen and the obscenities. Blast. I didn't want the extra paperwork, so I intended to give him a verbal flea in his ear and send him on his way, once he had binned the hats. He denied anything to do with the Shakespearian writing. Like I was born yesterday. His

Canadian accent threw me a bit - he was short with a wimpy build. Nothing like what I was used to and my 6'1" made me look like a bit of a giant beside him.

A discussion ensued at the end of which he gave me the pen so I could do a comparison of the ink colours. As I started to scribble on one of the hats, he ran off down the hill, at speed. The dog van rocked with Cara going nuts with her barking. "Boss, one was getting away!" I ran to the van and let her out as I saw our young man run across the intersection. I knew Cara was going to have problems because of her health but it was better than being on my own. I called out a couple of times for him to stop and guess what - he didn't.

The footpath was covered with low tree branches and the street lighting was almost non-existent. I got occasional glimpses of this little character running down the hill. I knew when he got down to the bottom, darkness would be his friend and my enemy. As I expected, Cara couldn't keep up. Her old weary bones just didn't operate as they did in her younger days.

At the bottom of the hill darkness was victor. I had no idea where he had gone. A few moments later Cara arrived and quickly went into the bushes on my right and started to bark. I called on him to come out and got no response. I bent over to go into the bushes and that was when size was irrelevant. I was off balance going into darkness. He grabbed me and pulled me down. Then he started to punch my upper left forearm. I thought don't you know anything about fighting; that was one of the most ineffectual places to hit someone. I could not believe this little runt of a person was trying to fight me. I lived, worked and breathed the streets;

they were the blood in my veins, my reason for getting out of bed each day. A street fighter would never do this - they were too smart to take on someone with such a size advantage.

Then I smelt fresh blood. It made no sense. I had done nothing to make him bleed. Next, I became aware of a new sensation, warm hot blood against my flesh. As a Night Shift Dog Handler, I just wear a thin Police jersey and regulation shirt. He must be bleeding very badly for it to come through my clothes.

I was angry and annoyed that this little twerp was causing so much bother over a few party hats. Did he have any idea how much paperwork was ahead of me when I got him back to the station - inconsiderate bugger!

On the street corner, the only street lighting bounced around in the tree branches and created an erratic symphony of light. In one movement, I got a glimpse of the blade of his knife. If anyone tells you they have stabbing pains, take it from someone who knows; they have no idea what they are talking about.

The knife quickly and silently entered my body once again. Now I knew why he was fighting as he was. It never registered with me that my left arm was not working. When I saw the blade a second time, I grabbed his wrist. I realized I had created a bigger problem for myself. I was obviously bleeding badly because the warm blood was into my crotch region and I didn't feel well. I couldn't hold hands forever; I didn't know how long this relationship would last. I had to let go and once again I never felt the silent entry. When the blade came back for its next attack, I grabbed and twisted it with all my strength until he let go. I then threw the knife as far as I could. (Later evidence in court showed I had only thrown it a few feet.)

I had to get him back to the Police Station. Did I forget to say this all took place within 100 yards? And did I also forget to say that I had not radioed off and told anyone what I was up too? Did I also forget to tell you I did not have my torch or radio with me, but I did have my handcuffs? I drove my knee into his back and with one hand forced his hands around until I handcuffed him. Sounds strange but as a Dog Handler you often catch offenders on your own with the dog. So, you had the dog on a leash, which used one hand, and you mastered techniques for hand cuffing offenders using the one free hand. It still had not registered with me that my left arm was not working. Cara has not come in because she was not allowed unless I commanded her. She was making an unholy racket of barking on the outside of the bushes.

The cold night air, the warm blood not trickling but flowing, runs down the inside of my trousers as I stood up. I grabbed him by the belt to lift him up and I planned to carry him to the cells. He was wimpy in size. I got him off the deck before I passed out. I was drifting in and out of consciousness. The irony did not escape me of how close I was to the station. This was one of my smaller offenders, and I was going to die on the roadside beside him. At this stage, I could have done with a TV director to make everything right.

Then it happened. As I drifted off again, I had a euphoric sense of peace and calmness. I looked back at my body beside the young man who wanted to terminate my life. Cara was doing her best to undress him, one set of ivory chunks at a time. A Police Dog is allowed to attack without command when the handler has been attacked, and I had stopped telling her not to come in. No, I wasn't capable of such a command.

I looked down at the scene, then looked away towards a light, and started to drift towards it. It felt extremely pleasant like no other experience I 'd had in my life. I didn't know why or how it happened, but I remembered my two daughters and I hadn't kissed them goodbye. I had to go back until I saw my daughters.

As I drifted in and out of consciousness, I realised the Ambulance was with me and all my colleagues were running around - their voices echoed apprehension as though they were preparing for my wake.

Somehow, the Ambulance got me to the Hospital – I was still drifting. They asked me where it hurt, and my only pain was with breathing. A Doctor made a sarcastic remark about it being in my head and instructed the nurse to cut my clothes off so they can examine me more fully.

The nurse started to cut my jersey and shirt away. She lifted my left arm to do the job and then as a punctured tyre quickly releases the pressure, so my lungs let go and the air screamed out. The medical staff now raised the intensity of their voices – I couldn't understand what was happening. Then I felt pain, without any anaesthetic, as the Doctor cut my back with a scalpel. They were driving pipes into my side and it hurt like hell.

The next moment I came around was in the X-ray as they rearranged my body for the pictures. I assured the radiologist that I couldn't smile. She told me I should not after the rough treatment in emergency. Then nothingness!

32

An era closes

Hospitals are vital places to start the healing process, but they are boring and full of sick people. The day arrived for my release and to get out of Hospital attire and into my own clothes excited me. Actually, my emotions were erratic. We lived in a Police house and luxury living it was not. The house was basic and pragmatic. This didn't worry me, what worried me was how Cara was going to react. We hadn't seen each other since the night of the stabbing.

I received reports she was fretting, and they were having trouble feeding her - this was totally out of character for her - she loved food. At one stage, the nurses were involved in a joint conspiracy with my wife to bring Cara into the Hospital and up the stairwell, so I could sneak out and see her. I put the brakes on this idea. I would love to see my companion, but I was struggling at every level: physically, emotionally and spiritually. I also worried about how excited she would be and how I would have to control her at a time when neither of us wanted those dynamics.

Even though it was only a few weeks in Hospital, getting into my own clothes felt exhilarating. My left arm was extremely weak as this was where most of the damage occurred. My left lung collapsed with the knife severing it and the hole where they put the lung drain in was one of the most uncomfortable wounds. My right hand was still bandaged from where I had ripped the knife off the pleasant little fellow who rearranged my body and life. Still freedom beckoned.

My daughters were not coming to pick me up. The oldest was at school and the youngest being cared for by a friend. I wanted them near me, but others were making decisions for me. Throughout the whole process, arrays of others made decisions for me, without involving me in the process at all. This added to the strange cacophony of psychological things swirling around in my head.

The drive from Hamilton to Te Awamutu where we lived felt tortuous. I couldn't adjust to the sensation of speed. All the drugs were still in my system and the fastest experience had been walking the ward. Cars came towards us at what felt like lightning speed. As we got close to Te Awamutu, I felt nauseous. I realised what poor quality our roads were in, each bump felt like a minor earthquake, shaking my tattered body in places it did not like.

The agreement with my wife was when we got home, she would leave me in the car and go to let Cara out of her kennel. The gated driveway was to separate us. She could easily jump the gate, but I hoped she would sense the situation and be gentle. I waited in the car, feeling both excited and trepidation at seeing my girl again.

Next thing I saw her bounding down the driveway towards the gate. Her tail wagging so fast I feared it might fly off. I got out of the car and wanted to run towards her, but my mind and body engaged in argument. The body won I was not capable of a fast walk. Cara jumped her front paws onto the gate and her face smiled a thousand smiles. I got to her and leant across the gate to pat her, even though I wanted to hug.

Cara knew I wasn't 100% and calmed herself down. I opened the gate and she came through. I lowered myself to the ground and just embraced her. She remained gentle, just wanting to feel my touch, as I did hers. I had no idea what the future held for either of us as the hierarchy had callous down to an art form. On my second day in Hospital, without explanation, they took my pup, Wal, away and I had no idea where he was. Cara knew I was upset and gently put her paw on my leg to console - no one or anybody knew and understood me like she did. We had been to hell together, not knowing if we had a return ticket.

Time was meaningless. It felt like eternity we sat together on the driveway, but it was probably minutes. I became aware of how tired I was feeling and went inside to rest. Cara went back to her kennel, happy to know she and the boss were reunited.

The next few weeks were about trying to rehabilitate my fitness levels. Cara never complained about the pace, it actually worked for her because of her own poor health. I got many visitors, which tired me, but the hardest part was no one knew what was going on inside of me. The offender was granted bail two days after my stabbing. The judge ruled there was no public safety involved, that it "was only a Policeman he attacked" were his reported words. His comments made me feel wonderful hearing the value of my life and job. I had to be a professional Policeman, but I felt like a victim. The picture for a nasty trial was brewing, but I couldn't talk to anyone about what was going on. Often Cara sat beside me, without judgement, just listening to me, but she was too close to this one for me to chat with her.

I was totally alone. My wife made it clear my stabbing was a no-go zone.

One day I got a phone call telling me when I was due back on duty. Every night I suffered terrible nightmares, reliving what happened. I woke up, sweating and shaking.

Cara and I started back on a night shift. Luckily, it was quiet, but three nights into the week, the duty Senior Sergeant asked us to back up an inexperienced beat Constable at a domestic dispute. I left Cara in the van as her presence could escalate such a situation.

The house was an old villa type building, demonstrating years of tenants as opposed to owners. The wooden front door with frosted inset windows was slightly open. I stood in the doorway and listened. The voices all sounded reasonably calm. I quietly went down the hallway towards the voices. As I entered the kitchen/dining room area, the young Constable was standing just inside the door. He looked out of his depth, eyes darting here and there, and twitching hands. Seated at the dining room table was a young woman, who looked in her mid-twenties. Standing with his back to the kitchen, facing us was a young, well-built guy, also mid-twenties. The conversation took a surprised jolt with my arrival.

I introduced myself, saying I was there to help. The young guy was standing against an open kitchen drawer. I edged my way towards him and slipped my right hand into my trouser pocket. There I slide my baton thong around my hand. I asked the young guy to move away from the drawer.

As quick as a flash I saw him pulling a large knife out of the drawer. I sprang forward with my baton out and whacked him across the hand with it. The knife crashed to the ground and I grabbed him, spinning him around to the floor. I bellowed at the Constable for his handcuffs. He struggled to pass them to me as he was shaking so much. Then voices in the corridor as the duty Sergeant arrived.

I left them to their arrest and went back to Cara in the dog van. I lost it. Uncontrollably crying. Cara looked through the window, in pain at watching the boss like this. It took some time to calm myself down. Luckily, we had no other incidents that night.

Over the next number of weeks, I went to another twenty-two knife incidents and two firearm ones. My nerves were completely shot. No one had caught me crying except Cara, and she was powerless to help.

Then on a Saturday night, Cara and I were dispatched to Morrinsville. A burglary at a local sports goods store activated the alarm and the offender decamped on foot with an array of guns and knives. The responsibility for catching him was Cara's and mine. The night shift Detective had a small side arm, accurate for about an inch past the end of the barrel. He offered to accompany me.

I was shaking and perspiring on this cold night. My stomach was a Gordian knot. I cast Cara around the front of the sports shop. Being the professional she was, her tail wagging she picked up the track and off we went across the main road. Down the footpath at speed and around the corner. Cara was in heaven, me in hell.

Past the shops and she headed into the first domestic section.

As she flew over a small fence, a flick of her head indicated our offender dropped an object. When I reached that point, I saw a large hunting knife on the ground. I pointed it out to the Detective and carried on. I knew for the sake of Cara I must operate at her speed. Another indication and a rifle on the ground. Cara was accelerating and her head rising. The lifting head meant we were gaining ground. My Gordian knot was getting tighter and nausea ravaged my insides. My shaking was getting worse and fear multiplying with every step. I grabbed my radio and requested the Armed Offenders. The duty Senior Sergeant refused.

I pulled the tracking line on Cara to slow her.

"You all right, mate?" the Detective questioned.

"Shitting myself - I can't do this."

I stopped Cara, said nothing, and took her out of her tracking harness, putting her onto the lead. She was puzzled but knew not to argue.

Saying nothing, I returned to the dog van and silently drove back to Hamilton Station. My career as a Dog Handler was over. The Senior Sergeant called for the Police Doctor; he injected me with something to knock me out. How Cara and I got home, I don't know.

The next week the Welfare Officer arrived to plan my exit. Handing back my uniform was gut-wrenching. My GP insisted I go to University and start a new life. My wife announced that our marriage was over so Cara and I bought a little cottage for us to be together.

One day I came home from Uni and she had soiled the house.

She looked upset and guilty. I rang the Vets.

"Her kidneys and liver are failing, Bruce."

"How long?"

"I don't know."

I took Cara home with a box of medications, but I knew the end was near. The medications were not working and two weeks later, after virtually no sleep, I took her back to the Vet. I asked my Minister to accompany me.

The Vet checked her out and just looked at me – no words. I insisted on holding her – we had been through too much to be apart at this stage. I took her home to our cottage and buried her at the back of the section.

It was all too much. I was suffering severe depression, on a truckload of pills and miserable. The time was over for self-pity and I needed to fix myself. I decided to admit myself to Tokanuii Psychiatric Hospital on the understanding that I was responsible for my own thoughts and actions. I was looking for tools, techniques to drag myself out of the mess I felt on the inside.

And so, a new chapter in my life began..

****

Epilogue

At University, I met the most wonderful woman, Suraya, who changed my life for the better.

Part two
The second dog collar

Shirley challenged me

I had been out of the Police for over a year, going to University, trying to get some qualifications for whatever the next stage of my life bought.

My head twirled as I reflected on how I lost the job I loved, my health, my marriage and somehow had been estranged from the two precious souls that brought me back from the precipice, my daughters.

My connection with the Church had been constant throughout my life, with Dad being an ordained Presbyterian Minister so I guess the apple fell near the tree.

The spiritual dynamics of my stabbing played a role in upping the ante of my Church life. I'd been taking Sunday School for a few years and engaged in youth work. Our Minister, Murray, asked me on behalf of the Church to become an elder and I agreed.

There was a wider Church conference at Morrinsville, and Shirley, another elder, and I were asked to represent our

Parish. We decided we would commute each day to the conference, from Te Awamutu. After the second day I was driving us back when Shirley asked me to stop the car. There was no urgency in her voice, in fact a calming tone, but also indicating there was something important on her mind.

I found a safe spot and parked the car. Shirley stayed looking out the front windscreen and she explained how a number of the Parish had been praying for me for some time. She and a few of the elders believed I was being called into ordained Ministry. I silently absorbed what she said.

As a teenager on an Easter Camp, near Matamata, I left the camp believing I was being called into Ministry, but equally knew I had other things to do first. Since my stabbing I'd spent a lot of time in reflection and thought and was wondering whether this was the time. Being true to myself, I hadn't discussed this with anyone, so Shirley's challenge came as no surprise at one level. The surprise for me was the timing. I still had all the inner turmoil of the drastic change in my life to sort out, and yet here were others seeing that the timing was right. I said I needed to think and pray about what she had said before I gave any response.

We did the next day at Morrinsville and Shirley carried on as though nothing had happened. She respected my need for space, thought and prayer.

A number of days later I asked her to accompany me to our Minister and gave my decision – even though I did not understand it, perhaps the time *was* right. Our Minister was 100% supportive and had been waiting for my visit.

That night I rang Mum and Dad, told them what had happened. Mum broke down in tears and Dad just said he was glad. My application went through the Church process, and it wasn't without challenges, mainly around whether I was well enough. The reservations of some were totally understandable, as I was wrestling with the very same issue. Was I stable enough?

University took on a new meaning now – I knew why I was there. The unexpected happened. I was bloody minded I was not getting back into another relationship and as a middle-aged single male at University, there was never a shortage of highly intelligent female friends. I had a group of married women, all of us similar age, doing same papers, and we all supported each other. We had study groups and I don't know how I would have coped if it wasn't for them.

As an aside, when I first started at Uni, I was so far out of my depth and comfort zone it was ridiculous. I was a school dropout, only ever passed one Sergeant's exam paper and that was because D/I Phil spent a huge number of hours coaching me, and even then, I only got 51%. So, my personal confidence at getting anywhere with all these bright people around me, felt farcical.

My very first assignment was in one of my history papers, and I didn't know what I was doing. Eventually the marked paper came back to me as an A-. I made an appointment with the lecturer to discuss "my grade." In many ways I wished it was videoed. I sat down in front of him and said I was unhappy with the grade. He looked at my work and said, he could not give me a higher grade, but I definitely deserved the given grade. The look on his face was priceless when I explained I wasn't after a higher grade, but rather a lower one. In all his years he had never had a student say their grade was too high. I explained I wasn't used to passing anything and he told me he hoped I would get used to the experience.

In the last semester I started a new paper, New Zealand History. My driver in choosing my papers was mainly based around lecture times, so I could get a structure to my week that I wanted, rather than developing a strong degree. One of the assignments was a group presentation, so I teamed up with a number of my friends as we had similar interests and knew how to work well together.

Then one day I was climbing the stairs to the library to do research when a female voice called out from behind. I did not recognise the voice but turned around and about four steps below was this beautiful woman, whom I recalled from one of my other History papers. We had never spoken, but she came and asked if I could help her out. She was going to Auckland Uni the next year to do a Post Graduate Diploma in Broadcast and she had to have an A- average throughout her degree to be accepted. She was very slow at getting herself a group for the assignment and was worried about what their end quality of work would be like. Laurie, the lecturer, told her to approach me to help because "he was one of the best researchers I have encountered at undergraduate level, but equally was one of the worst writers." He suggested to Suraya that she could offer to help me with my writing, if I helped her with the research. I quickly agreed, on the grounds I knew my poor-quality writing was costing me a lot in grades.

When she asked what I was studying towards, it felt good to say that the following year I was going to Otago University to train to be a Presbyterian Minister. She surprised me with the quality of support – I was expecting her to walk away from a religious nutter.

Researching, writing, debating together lead to the obvious outcome – we became an item.

As the University year was drawing to a close, my emotions started to run high. I was already deeply in love with Suraya, and yet next year she was heading to Auckland Uni and I to Otago. I was also nervous about the fact that Otago was "old school" placing huge importance on exams, whereas Waikato was 100% internal assessment. I was pulling in ok grades, which had picked up under Suraya's tutorial work on my writing skills.

I decided to have a chat with my History Professor who took me for my Russian History papers. I loved his lectures and he teased me more than once that I would be the first student to read every library book on Russian History – I just loved the subject and couldn't get enough of it.

Prof Jensen was brilliant with me and suggested some teaching staff to make contact with when I got down to Otago – he also heard my concerns about my ability to disintegrate in an exam room and gave me some good tips.

Everything was set for the new venture. At our local service station, one of the young guys told me he was going to Otago next year, and since I had managed to score a flat to live in, having a group of other Uni students as flat mates felt good.

The farewell with my daughters and Suraya was painful, but I got in my car to drive all the way to Otago and start the process of learning how to wear "back to front" shirts (Minister humour for dog collars).

34

Otago

My furniture arrived at the flat the day before I did, so when I reached the flat, Colin and his girlfriend had already moved in. They were worried they might have taken the room I wanted, but the room they left for me was perfect.

My first day at Knox (the school of Theology for Otago Uni) was an anxious one for me. Even though I was training to be a Minister, I was uncomfortable around real "holy rollers." We had to enrol, and the Principal was keen for me to do a Bachelor of Divinity, because I was far enough through my BA to allow it to happen. When I discovered this would mean me doing Hebrew & Greek, I shut down. Languages have never been my strong point – four years of studying French at College and never managing to make double figures in the tests, etc., was too big a hurdle for me to overcome. So, I managed to get permission to do a Bachelor of Theology in Church History and finish my Bachelor of Arts in Russian History. A tough three years was looming.

University was (and still was) an exciting place for me. I am like blotting paper, excited to learn new things, challenge my personal thinking and dogma, find new world views. It was a true sheltered workshop for intellectuals (not that I consider myself an intellectual).

I loved Dunedin. It was a picturesque city, wonderful architecture, a strong sense of Scottish history and the birthplace of the Presbyterian Church. I missed Suraya, but this was overcome by daily writing to her about what I had been up to and then we rang each other after ten at night. Tolls were cheaper at that time of night and two broke students, couldn't afford to fritter away their funds.

My favourite subjects were the history ones, but I knew the pragmatic reason for studying the other papers, such as Old and New Testament Theology, Systematic Theology and Pastoral studies. I was starting to form new friendships (I am by nature a strong introvert and it often takes me a long time to form friendships). Tony and I were becoming good mates. He was a young married man and Joy was expecting their first child. We all got on brilliantly. Part of the dynamics was everyone trying to decide what was each other's theological stance. I aligned myself with the "liberals" because I saw this as the group that would give me the most freedom to explore, searching for deeper meaning. Dad's books all reinforced his conservative stance, whereas for me I did not want to be locked into any one school of thought.

Tony appeared to be in a similar situation, so we had many wonderful hours debating and discussing different theological perspectives. Every Wednesday we had a Chapel service that was taken by students, on a voluntary basis. We had Chapel every day, but for us first years, our allocated day was Wednesday. Easter was drawing near and so I spoke to Tony about the two of us taking a service together. Experimentation was the norm and I was like a dog dying of thirst discovering a bucket of water.

Tony and I went to one of the beaches and found a couple of old branches from a tree. We used old stuff and joined them into a hardcase, rugged cross. We had music, etc., that tied it all together. What we were not prepared for was the last part of the service where we had a couple of hammers with two buckets of rusty nails. We had everyone singing the hymn "Were you there when they crucified my Lord." Tony and I, armed with a hammer each, took a rusty nail and hammered it into our cross. Without saying anything we went to the "congregation" and tried to pass on the hammer. Most shunned the offer. Eventually another two took our hammers, with tears running down their cheeks did the same as us. My guess was about 50% participated, but there no words spoken. Tony did an ancient blessing to wrap it up, and it was a while before anyone got up to leave the Chapel.

The lecturers used what happened in Chapel for a few weeks to get their classes to analyse what happened and why. The exercise taught me the power of creativity in worship, but also caution because symbolism can open wounds in others in very unexpected ways, and if this happens there was a need to have appropriate pastoral care mechanisms in place.

I always loved it when the Pacific Island communities led Chapel – the singing was inspirational and moving. The hard part was running down the hill after Chapel to go to one of my Russian History papers, not because I didn't want to be there, but it broke the mood, almost instantly.

There was a part of me feeling like a schizophrenic, walking in the theological world, and then with the everyday University world. They felt like two separate worlds. Somehow, the Church had created its own bubble, isolating it from the reality of what every day folk were/are experiencing. This dynamic played a role in shaping what sort of Parish Minister I wanted to be. I never saw myself as a "holy roller" but did see myself as a spiritual human, experiencing such things as the night of my stabbing. The death tunnel that night was not (from my perspective) a religious experience, but rather a spiritual experience.

Hence, my whole time at Knox, I felt, at certain levels, like an outsider, but at the same time relishing the experience I was going through. I knew that sooner or later, some of my "thinking/views" would be exposed, and I was right.

Attending tutorials was an essential part of the University culture/way of life. I always felt that those who skipped them missed a huge component of the richness that was academic life. But I guess that depended on why you were there.

I often stayed silent through a lot of tutorials, simply because I liked to assimilate a lot of the various views. Our New Testament tutorial was discussing the apostle Paul, and I was giving myself strong messages to keep my trap shut. After a couple of weeks on this subject the tutor challenged me. "Bruce, I notice you are extremely quiet on this subject, was there a reason?"

It felt like a checkmate question. I squirmed and wormed with different answers, but she would not give up on me. I explained there would be a number present who would find my opinions and thoughts on Paul offensive, and for some potentially bordering on heresy, therefore I preferred to remain silent. What I thought would bring the subject to an end, did the complete opposite. The group virtually demanded to know what I thought.

I struggled within myself to work how to word what I wanted to say – Police training had me as a forthright speaker, not one for mincing my words. This situation required a form of delicacy I was not strong in.

So I explained to the group, that if I met this Apostle Paul on the street, and if he babbled on like he did in his writings, I would eventually bop him on the end of his nose for being an arrogant little twerp. Being in a gentle state of mind, I continued to explain that I was sick of the Church worshipping Paul, rather than God. Then I sat back and waited for crucifixion without resurrection.

It was fair to say there was a lengthy silence, and my fellow students were looking to the tutor for first reaction. She was an extremely good diplomat and kept everyone's tonsils still within them and used what I had said as a discussion starter for the following weeks. When the tutorial finished, she asked could she have a word with me. Here we go, I thought. She waited until all the other students had left and then told me she also thought there were sections of the Church who worshipped Paul rather than God. She also pleaded with me to keep coming back as she thought the class needed an injection of challenge. I agreed to come to the next tutorial, but only lasted a few more as I felt like the proverbial leper.

In fairness, the environment allowed for a huge amount of debating and challenging, but I was not keen to express fully what I was wrestling with on the inside.

My wrestling continued when I did the paper "The Church and the Third Reich," which explored the role of the Church during Nazi Germany. The role of the Church and politics was constantly debated, but the horror for me was when I learnt some Churches hung the Swastika in their Church, because from their perspective, this was the flag of Germany. I still struggle with the concept of Nationalism, flags, etc., because although it can bring people together, it was also used to justify appalling behaviour.

During this paper I encountered the written works of Dietrich Bonhoeffer, a Pastor in the Lutheran Church in Germany during the 1930's – and part of the 40's. Bonhoeffer was a staunch pacifist, because he could not align the Bible with being pro-war, in fact he strongly believed the Gospels spoke more about pacifism that pro-war. I totally got where he was coming from. After my stabbing I became very anti-violence.

Bonhoeffer captured me with his now book "Letters and Papers from Prison." He had played a (minor) role in the assassination attempt on Hitler's life. His papers are a journey of him wrestling with the dynamic of being a pacifist, but how do you deal with something as evil as Adolf Hitler and his regime. To cut a long story short, he hoped no one else would ever be in the position he was, and he never wanted anyone to take even a minor role in taking another life. He was captured by the Gestapo for his role and executed only days before the war ended. A great theologian, his life cut short before he had really got started.

This paper captured me for a whole range of reasons, and I felt at a basic level I connected with Bonhoeffer – I am not academic enough to have his theological insights, but I connected as a fellow human wrestling on their journey.

No one was more surprised than me, when at the end of three years at Dunedin I had successfully obtained two undergraduate degrees. Not bad for a thicko from school days!

Suraya and I were married at Hamilton on my middle year. We married at the University of Waikato Chapel. We literally prepared everything for our wedding from Dunedin, we jointly wrote the script for our service, flew up a few days before and back to Dunedin the day after. We joked for years that our honeymoon was holding hands on the flight back.

Suraya had finished at University of Auckland with a post graduate Diploma in Broadcast Communication and had landed a job as a trainee director on Playschool, filmed in Dunedin. I personally got to know Big & Little Ted and some of the other stars. Halfway through my last year, TVNZ did what they were very proficient at doing, restructured, and she lost her job. Her dream had been stolen from under her. There were very nasty politics through the whole process, but we relied on her income. It was a very stressful time for both of us, but especially her. She managed to get herself a job as a Producer at Massey University Television Production Unit, so once again we were separated.

The end of the University year said it was time to find a Parish, which was easier said than done. Everyone wants experienced clergy, not one wet behind the ears. With Suraya living in Palmerston North, I went to Nan, my mentor from the teaching staff. Nan was always 100% supportive of me, and she was incredibly wise. She told me St Marks in Palmerston North was vacant and she knew the interim moderator extremely well. She proposed I fly up in the last break, take a service there, so both parties could check each other out. I readily agreed and contacted Paul, the Interim Moderator. He set the wheels in place for me to take a service, but in fairness, left it to me to take a service that reflected what my style of ministry would be.

In due time I drove to Palmerston North, both to catch up

with Suraya and to take the Church service. After a wonderful reunion, I returned to Dunedin. I was wrapping up my studies for two degrees, but also had to finish the Church requirements for my Diploma of Ministry, so my last term was a blur with my head buried in books. I was also looking after our youngest son who was at primary school. We decided it would be the least disruptive to him if he stayed with me as I could work my University life around him much easier than Suraya could her working life.

After exams, Paul told me St Marks wanted to "call me" (this was Church language for taking you to the next stage of recruitment). I obviously accepted, so now I had to return to the Waikato Presbytery, who had put me up for training, and I was to be ordained as a Minister. I now officially had my second dog collar.

35

Parish Ministry

The rituals of the Church can appear really weird, strange to those not accustomed to their ways. At my ordination in Hamilton, I was allowed to wear my robes and clerical collar. The next phase was to be inducted into a Parish and for me this was to be St Marks. Mum and Dad and some of my siblings came to this special ritual, and I actually felt for the first time in my life that my father was very proud of me.

The Church house (manse) was at the back of the Church, so accommodation was not an issue for us. It wasn't very far to the Primary School for Leif to attend, so life was clicking into place.

Now I had to get into the discipline of writing a sermon every week – the equivalent of a University assignment and appear fresh. The people of St Marks were very welcoming, and I had no idea what was going on behind our backs.

When Suraya and I got married we were both strongly of the opinion she would keep her own surname. The Parish accepted us with this knowledge, and that she was a professional woman who had a career and therefore could not, would not be a traditional Minister's wife. The Parish viewed themselves as very liberal, so this was no issue, so we thought.

When Suraya and I were at University of Waikato, a certain lecturer introduced us to each other. He had, previously to his life in academia, been a Presbyterian Minister, and his only Parish had been St Marks. The Parish members were delighted when they found this connection.

I quickly got into Minister routines, as there was a huge amount of personal discipline in the work. I had to plan, structure my week, otherwise Sunday would arrive and nothing was prepared. I am the most unmusical (if there was such a word) person you can meet. I am tone deaf and have no natural sense of timing. St Marks was a dream for me, because not only was there a Choir, there was a team of organists.

I very quickly developed a rapport with the organists, giving them plenty of warning what the theme for the service was and they would select the music for the service. A total win/win of playing to our own strengths. A bit further down the track I set up a worship committee, which was a brilliant way of getting greater depth into the services.

My stabbing had made me very curious about the whole death and dying scenario, so during my University years I had read everything I could on the subject and became a fan of Elizabeth Kubler-Ross's work. Dad had advised me to get to know the funeral directors really quickly so I decided I was going to visit the two local firms in the one day. I turned up at the first one, a very formal, polite meeting and a quick look through his Chapel.

I then went to the second firm, explained who I was and that I wanted them to get to know me. The office lady got Colin to come out and meet me, and he was thrilled that I was making myself known. We chatted and then he offered to show me around. We went through the Chapel and then out the back. When we got to their mortuary, he opened the door and there was Brent trying to lift a body onto the slab. As quick as lightening Colin closed the door. I protested, saying the guy inside looked like he needed a hand. Colin was flummoxed but saw something in my look that he took seriously. He opened the door and introduced me to Brent. Between us was the deceased and neither Funeral Directors knew where to look.

I forgot myself and just said to Brent I would lift the feet if he took the other end. He nodded and we lifted the body onto the slab. I carried on talking throughout and asked what the next stage of the process was. Remove the clothing for the embalming process. So, I just carried on conversing while helping sort the deceased out. Brent just accepted I was comfortable with what was happening, but Colin was still speechless. Eventually he blurted out "What was your past, because in all my years I have never had a Minister do what you have done." At first, I was puzzled and then explained I was a former street cop and had dealt with many dead bodies. Both of them noticeably relaxed and Colin went and made us a cup of tea while I carried on helping Brent.

Afterwards I chatted with them about what help was available for families after the funeral and was not surprised to discover none. I explained I wanted to set up a "grief support group" and although I intended to run it at the Church, it was open to anyone. I think, but I could be wrong, that my matter of fact approach hit a chord with them, and they sent a lot of people to our group.

I announced in the pulpit one week, as well as having a notice in the bulletin, I intended to start up a grief support group. We would meet monthly, with a shared lunch. And so, started one of the greatest privileges in my life.

Each month we would meet, everyone bringing food for a shared lunch. Each session I provided an article on grief for the following session with questions I wanted everyone to think about. The group became very close, but always welcoming for new people. I only asked one person to leave, a widower who (it was quickly obvious) was there to find a new wife and was upsetting some of the group with his advances.

One Sunday, I was standing out front shaking everyone's hand (as you do) and Belle asked me if she could have a private word. I wasn't sure what it was all about, and she suggested we walk out onto the lawn away from everyone else's hearing. If she was comfortable with this suggestion, so was I. Belle had been one of the inaugural members of our grief support group. When we were out of hearing of all the others, she explained that she has been asked by other members of the Parish to have a "pastoral" word with me. What happened next made me grateful for all my years in the Police. She told me how the Parish were really enjoying my Ministry and they thought Suraya was lovely, but they had a wee favour to ask – would we consider getting married. My mind was in overdrive as to how to answer her question, so I explained that I would need to talk this through with Suraya and I would let her know within a month.

She walked back to the Church and was quickly surrounded by a number of the other ladies. I wide berthed them, not to cause discomfort, all the time inwardly smiling to myself.

Over lunch I explained to Suraya what had happened, and she quickly retorted "well I hope you told her we are?" I said no because I needed the whole Parish to know at the same time, to knock speculation/gossip on the head.

Four weeks later, we held a planned service to celebrate "family." All our other kids were down for the school holidays and so we made a banner for them to carry into the Church on Sunday.

The service started normally, and I was at the front and the families were to carry in their banners and put them across the front of the sanctuary. Towards the end, our kids were coming in with wide smiling faces, carrying our banner. In the middle of the banner was one of my favourite photos of our wedding. All our kids were in our bridal party ('reconstituted marriage' was the phrase) and for us, the kids being at it was huge. And yes, my two daughters were at our wedding and at this service. I could not take my eyes off Belle. They were wide open, and her jaw was bouncing. Nothing was said that day or ever since, but there was a noticeably relaxed atmosphere going on within the Church – their Minister had a new legitimacy.

Over lunch, we discussed this as a family, and everyone in their own way commented about how cool it was that the Parish had accepted me as their Minister, believing that Suraya and I weren't married. Church people often get judged for a whole lot of reasons, but St Marks had, in their silence and inaction, shown unconditional love to both Suraya and me. They went up a number of rungs in my mind for having been so accepting.

The grief support was strong and the information that I was legitimately married, relaxed us all. One Monday, as I was preparing to go across to the group, I got a call that my ex-wife's boyfriend had dropped dead while out marathon running on the Sunday. With this news twirling in my mind, I went to the group.

One of the group, commented that I had a funny look on my face, what was behind it. I commented "I now know there is a God" and got even more quizzical looks. I explained about the call I had received. There was a ripple of smiles as they joined the dots to my God statement. I then (being in a naughty mindset) said I have often struggled with the concept of heaven and hell, now it made sense. After I die, whichever wife I meet will symbolically tell me whether I am in heaven or hell. The group burst out laughing. I was now a true human, not some God in human clothes.

36

Weddings are times of celebration

Weddings are times of celebration, hope, laughter, family and friends acknowledging two people making a statement of intention for their relationship.

St Marks Church was a hall on the side of a large section. When the new Parish was established in the burgeoning new suburb, the long-term goal was to build a new place of worship on the vacant land. The hall was plain and only the cross on the street front indicated it was a Church. Hence, it was not a traditional Church, attracting numerous weddings.

The inside was as plain as the outside; two columns of pews facing a sanctuary two steps above the congregation. In the sanctuary was a large wooden communion table with a lectern on one side, organ and Choir seating on the other. A wedding in this setting was about community.

Jane and Michael were not members of our congregation but knew of our passion for the people in Awapuni. I had a number of meetings with them as we prepared a service, just for them. Every wedding service was different – it had to reflect the couple and have special meaning for them.

On the Friday night before the main event, we gathered with the full bridal party for the rehearsal. This ensured everyone knew where to stand and what was going to happen. Rehearsals are fun, light-hearted affairs to try and keep everyone in good shape for the next day. Things can go wrong, but because every service written was for that particular couple, no one knows if something did not go exactly according to the original plan.

Jane and Michael were a lovely young couple. She was a bubbly effervescent twenty-two-year-old brunette, just 5'5" in height. Michael was the subdued, more thoughtful one of the two, showing his extra two years of age. Both of them were very responsible and it was special when they gaze into each other's eyes, reflecting their adoration and love.

Jane had one sister and a cousin as attendants – Michael a friend as best man and brother as attendant. The three-year-old flower girl, Holly, with her curly blonde hair and dimple in her chin was a picture of cuteness. Nathan, the four-year-old was the ring bearer. Typical of a four-year-old he asked dozens of questions, demonstrating a mind that was ready for school, before the system was prepared to have him.

I took them through the process a couple of times to make sure everything flowed nicely. Jane had arranged for the rings to be tied to a cushion so that Nathan couldn't lose them. I always had lollies and toys in the sanctuary for bridal party children, to slow down the risk of them getting quickly bored.

I arrived at the Church about thirty minutes before the service and got into my robes. Michael and his party arrived ten minutes before start time. They looked dashing in their sharp grey trousers, with matching waistcoats, white shirts, blue and gold striped ties. One-minute feels like an hour for the males so I never wanted them there too early.

I checked with the best man to make sure he had the required hammer and six-inch nails. I got a quizzical look. They are to nail Michael's feet to the floor if there was risk of him running. I explain to Michael not to panic if Jane didn't arrive on time; it means either she was late or not coming. Michael didn't know whether to laugh or cry.

The Church was filling up with the invited guests. I told the men I was going down to greet Jane – the next time they saw me it meant she has arrived, unless I look perplexed and it meant disaster.

I'd just reached the front of the Church in time to see the silver Holden wedding cars arriving. The first one carried the bridesmaids and they alighted quickly. They looked beautiful in their aqua blue gowns and posies with irises. Nathan got out looking like a miniature version of the male attendants and Holly a miniature version of the bridesmaids.

The next car had Jane and her father. Jane had a low-cut lacy gown with a light aqua blue sash. Her hair was done in twirls with irises weaved through them. She was sensational!

The photographer did his thing and then I walked into the Church and gave the organist the nod. She played Bette Midler's "Wind beneath my wings" as the bridal party progresses down the short aisle. Michael had teary eyes and he smiled at his bride. Dad passed Jane over to Michael and we were into the formal part of the service. I glanced down at Holly and Nathan – both were having a little party with the lollies and toys.

As we started the vows, I gave the best man the signal to get the rings off the cushion. He started to turn towards Nathan and then we heard the sound of metal on wooden floor.

Tinkle, tinkle, tinkle... silence. I glanced across. The rings had dropped into a crack in the floor. The best man knelt down and tried to get them out. They were stuck. He gave me a quizzical look. I reached under my robes and got a pen out of my shirt pocket. I gently leaned down towards him and passed the pen. The front row attendees started to giggle.

He slipped the pen between the first ring and the floor. No movement. He tried the second ring – same result. The time had now arrived when I was supposed to bless the rings. It wasn't hot, but I started to sweat. Jane was looking like she was going to burst into tears, Michael into laughter.

Then I remembered I was wearing two rings. Quickly as I could I slipped of my wedding and signet rings. Smiling at Michael and Jane the whole time, they realised what I was up to, as did the best man. He rapidly got back into place and made out as if he was placing the rings on my folder. Both rings were far too big for Michael and Jane, but they held them on to keep the illusion. At long last we got to the procession out of the Church.

I shot out the back door to the kitchen where I knew there was a screwdriver. I used it as a chisel and eventually managed to get the rings out. I then, discreetly, went outside to congratulate the couple and swap the rings, so I had my own back. Only a few of the guests had any idea of what had gone wrong, but Michael and Jane had an eternal memory of their wedding.

37

No one told me about the power of life and death

Everyone in the Parish was equal but some more equal than others (playing with Orwell's words from 'Animal Farm'). Ngariki was one such person. She was a Pacific Islander married to a pakeha. An elder at the Church, you would never find a more loving, wonderful woman than her. She told me apologetically that her husband, Andy, was not a "Churchgoer." I told her it wasn't an issue and not to worry about it.

I used to spend a decent amount of time each week visiting Parishioners and I always loved visiting her. Andy was there and we quickly developed a great bond. He was a retired freezing worker, a real down to earth, good bugger. One day Ngariki rang me and asked could I come and visit them both that day, to which I quickly agreed.

As soon as I walked into the dining room, I knew something was wrong. Ngariki did the talking and told me their only son had died of misadventure a few years before I arrived. I had heard about it, but never pried. She took me through what happened and how when he died, it felt to her that he took a chunk of her heart with him, that she never felt whole again. What she was saying made sense, but I didn't know where the conversation was going. My job was just to listen and be there. After a while she was getting teary again, telling me her son's story obviously was a tearful time. These new tears were not for her son, so I just waited until she told me in her own way. She and Andy had been at the Doctor that morning and Andy's cancer (which I knew nothing about) had significantly expanded and he did not have very long to go.

No amount of training prepares you properly for a situation like this. I looked at Andy, and his eyes were swelling, but he was not going to cry. He saw me looking at him and moved his eyes to his wife. I knew what he was saying – look after my wife. The three of us spent a few hours together and I went home heavy hearted. Theoretically, I was meant to be emotionally separate, but these were two wonderful people who I cared deeply for, so I did what any self-respecting Scottish Presbyterian Minister would do, I had a dram of Malt whiskey, saluting them in silence.

Over the weeks Andy deteriorated at a fast pace. He was to stay in the marital bed, a wish of both of them. Every day I went and visited, sometimes just for a few minutes, other times longer. One morning my phone rang, and it was Ngariki saying she didn't know when I would be around, but could I come now. I didn't hesitate and was there a few minutes later. The Doctor had been earlier, and Andy was on his second day in a coma. There was nothing more he could do for him. I just hugged her, in silence, words seemed a violation of what was happening. Then Ngariki spun me out with what she said.

"Bruce, you have to go to Andy and tell him he has to die, it is time this was all over." No one at the theological hall told us about this type of situation. She would not come down the hall with me, and it was obvious I was not to come out until it was all over. I get emotional as I remember this, because it was tough.

I went down to the bedroom and sat on the chair beside Andy. I gently picked up his hand and held it. I had no idea what to do, and then I realised I had to go inside myself to find the solution. Holding his hand, even though he was in a coma, I asked him was he afraid to die because of leaving Ngariki on her own. His hand twitched. I asked a few more questions and got answers to those through his hands. I cannot to this day explain why or how I did it, I prayed for him to let go of life, and let those of us left to look after Ngariki. I looked down at my hands and they were still, but my inside was not. Who am I to tell another person to let go of life?

Time was still, the silence shouting at me, what had I just done. I didn't know how long it was, but Andy slowly released my hand as he left this life. It was a very peaceful death, and I said some prayers for him before I put his arm under the blanket, tidied him up a bit and went out the door. I slowly walked down the hallway to the dining room. I could hear Ngariki's voice, she was on the telephone, starting to tell the relatives that Andy had died. How that loving wife had the strength and courage to ring the phone chain she had set up a few weeks earlier still amazed me, but that she did, with my making her a cup of tea and just being there. We waited until the funeral director came and the two of us helped him take Andy's body.

The coffin was back in the house within a few hours, an open one with Andy in the middle of the lounge. The floor was covered in fine mats as a genuine tribute to this man she loved. Every time new visitors arrived, I was to be there to take prayers for them. It was one week my clerical collar never came off.

I arrived one morning and saw the lid placed on the coffin. I was puzzled as to why this had happened as I knew it was contrary to her culture. I managed to get her to one side and quietly asked why the lid was back on.

The Grandkids had been down the end bedroom playing games and wanted Granddad to join in, so they came down and took him out of the coffin to have him in the room with them. The adults explained to the kids it was preferred to leave Granddad in his coffin and the decision was made to cover him for one night so the kids would understand.

The day of the funeral arrived, and I had been at the house since just before dawn, as the busloads from all over New Zealand started to arrive. I took numerous mini services with each group and then late morning I took a service in the house, all in Ngariki's native language that before this week I had not spoken a word. During the week she had trained me what to do and say.

After the home service, the funeral director arrived to pick up Andy and take him to the Church for the "public funeral service." I did the majority of this in English, but out of respect did parts of it in Ngariki's native language.

After it was all over, I was back at their house and Ngariki explained (in her gentle way) that it was time for me to leave so it was just family left. I went home and did my Scottish tradition with my wee malt. The whole week had gone, and I still had a Sunday service to prepare.

The service on Sunday was us as a Church paying tribute to Ngariki and Andy, and how she epitomised the unconditional love of God.

A few years later I told Dad about this funeral, and he said he had spent his whole ministry career in fear of being called to do what I did, and luckily it never happened to him. My second time doing the same was for my father, dying with cancer, and helping him let go.

People can and have quoted to me all sorts of verses from the Bible about what happened. Perhaps I shouldn't say it, but for me they were expressing that they had no understanding of what happened, especially for me on the inside. I learnt a huge amount about myself through Andy and Ngariki, but more importantly for me, I learnt to be silent and let God do the talking.

I also started the learning process about the concept of the will to live, and the will to die. Technically, Andy should have died a week earlier, according to the Doctor, but he stayed. Some people pull the plug on themselves quickly when told they have cancer or some such potentially fatal illness. Others stay alive for some event that was important to them, and then very quickly die. I have never read anything of substance that explains the concept of the will to live/die, but I know most Ministers go through experiences where they see science play a back seat to the mind of the individual.

38

Teenagers, designed to destroy parents

One of my Parishioners asked after Church if she could set up a time to see me during the week. Of course, I was available, and like all such requests I had no idea what it would be about.

On the Wednesday she arrived promptly at the agreed time at my study. Our Church house was at the back of the Church, and I had a lovely office off the lounge room. I made a mandatory cup of tea and we sat down in the office. I could tell she was nervous, by the not being able to stay still, and the rapid voice, which was unusual for her. Usually I allow silence for the person to explain to me what was happening, but on this occasion, I expressed concern that she was stressed and asked her what was wrong.

She was concerned that their fifteen-year-old son was "hanging out" with a bad crowd. He answered his parents back, was permanently grumpy and had no regard for how he looked. Sounded like an average teenage boy to me. But the parents were extremely loving, caring, patient people and she was genuinely struggling.

We chatted for about an hour, and she seemed a lot calmer, so we brought our time together to a close. After she left, I reflected on how many of our Parish have teenagers. We had a strong youth group and her son was one of them – well he was until he started to hang out with these new friends.

What the mother didn't know was that I had had a very close and personal dealings with her son the weekend before. Our bedroom was right beside the Church and I was woken in the early hours one night by a car doing wheelies on the Church lawn. I dragged myself out of bed and could see the car getting ready to burn rubber on our beautifully manicured lawns. I forgot my new career and reverted back to my old.

I pulled on a pair of jeans and a sweatshirt and snuck down to the back door where my gumboots were. I slipped the gumboots on, snuck up the side of the house, using the Church as a barrier so they would not see me. When I got to the wall of the Church hall, the car was facing away from me, so using the shadows I crept up the side of the hall. The car proceeded to do another wheelie. It was obvious by the lack of proper control, that the driver had no decent skill at controlling the vehicle through such manoeuvres. The car window was lowered, so I crouched down, ready to spring. Sure enough the car stalled, only about fifteen feet away from me, but the car was facing away, so I sprang, ran up to the driver's door, put my hand through and grabbed the driver by the scruff of the neck.

He was coming out the window, whether he wanted to or not. What surprised me was how easily I pulled him through the window; I hadn't lost my old techniques. When he was about half out, he screamed at me to let him go, this was "his Church." I let him go and then he turned around. Yes, he was from our Church, and I didn't know at this stage that his mother would be in my office the following week.

I explained my disappointment in my young fellow, and he got very upset. To protect the not so innocent, I agreed not to do anything official about what had happened and would not tell his parents, provided he came and saw me once a week for the next two months. He was also to disassociate with his "mates," or else I would reverse my decision about his parents and official action.

So, after the mother left my office, I wondered what sort of a hard time the other parents were having. Doing nothing was never a choice to me, so the following Sunday I announced I was considering setting up a "Parents of Teenagers" support group and invited those interested to come to the Church Hall that Thursday night.

After the service, I got no reaction to my announcement, so when the Thursday came, I mentally decided no one would show up. After an early dinner, I wandered over to the hall to open it up, for my non-crowd. My non-crowd was thirty parents. I had nothing prepared, and to be honest no idea how it would all operate.

We all sat in a circle, after arming ourselves with the compulsory cup of tea and biscuit. I explained that this group was not about religion, but rather about parents feeling very alone while taking their young people through the tumultuous teenage years. Now it was up to them as to how they wanted it to operate.

After two hours, it was hard to get them all to leave – I was out every night with meetings, and I needed to have some degree of home life. The group set themselves a monthly meeting night, and just wanted to share what was going on for them. As the group got traction, they had all agreed they would never tell their kids what was discussed, and the young people got concerned about what was being said about them. The group code of silence became its most powerful voice and over time some families left, and new ones came. It was wonderful.

39

Writing sermons was a mammoth task

Writing sermons was a mammoth task. I didn't enjoy writing and having to come up with something new and relevant each week was hard work. Anything for a distraction. Hallelujah. The phone rangs. It was Brent, the funeral director. He had a difficult one for me.

The now deceased was mowing his lawns when he dropped dead. Instead of running for an Ambulance, the neighbour rang the family. Brent was with them at the deceased's house and they were fighting over the will. The deceased was still on the lawn, as they would not let Brent remove the body until the will "issues" were resolved. A Doctor certified death, plus cause. The deceased had a long bad cardiac history, so the heart attack was no surprise to the Doctor.

The address was not far from my home office so off I went. The family didn't belong to our Church, but Brent had used me for a few difficult funerals. Because of my former Police life, I seem to be able to handle them.

I got to the address within minutes and alighted from the car.

I could hear a male and female voice profusely swearing at each other. Brent was standing at the door, once he registered I'd arrived he physically relaxed.

"Good luck with this one," he grimaced as he commented.

I entered the dining room and here was a woman in her early thirties, her face screaming with rage. She was dressed in jeans and grey sweatshirt. The other party, obviously the brother, appeared slightly older, in a dark suit with an open neck white shirt. His face twisted with anger.

"Just what we want, a bloody religious nutter," the brother sneered.

I ignored him, went to the kitchen, and put the kettle on. I came back, formally introduced myself and explained a wee bit about my past. I then told them that Brent taking the body had no implications on the settlement of any will. In fact, a vitriolic sibling could use their current performance against them. The tactic worked; they both calmed down. I found out how they liked their tea and set them up around the table.

Then the rules of engagement were explained. Their father, no matter what, deserved the dignity of a decent funeral. We were going through the funeral process like mature adults and they could war over the will later through lawyers, knowing that the lawyers will come out best, but that was their choice.

I didn't think either of them were used to being spoken to as I had done. My attitude towards them did not portray their stereotype of what a Minister was supposed to be like. Now that the culture shock was having the desired effect, I started to ask questions about their father's life history. I didn't want to get into the funeral arrangements too quickly for fear of creating another world war.

When one gave an answer or told an anecdotal story the other disagreed with, I shut the objector. Everyone was entitled to his or her perspective of a story. Abusing the other was banned. After about an hour of letting them do most of the talking, the thing that registered with me was the lack of emotion as they talked about both their childhood and father. The only thing they showed any emotion over was money and what they perceived as their right.

I looked around the dining room for clues as to the family history. Usually there are photos to get people talking about, but these were absent. The room had a plain old oak dining table with four oak chairs. The carpet was too faded to draw any conclusion from. The plain old oak china cabinet was pragmatic, but devoid of clues. Both the wallpaper and curtains were old and faded. Everything about the room was tired. There was nothing about family, or their mother, which was unusual.

The ice was broken enough and so I asked about their mum. She died about ten years earlier after a rough time with cancer. Dad just shut down, would not talk about her and made the house devoid of memories. Everyone grieves differently.

Another blank wall except I was receiving clues as to how this family operated emotionally. I then started to ask about the funeral arrangements. Brent had made the most of the opportunity and removed the deceased from the lawn and the neighbour had put the motor mower back in the shed.

I took a lot of non-religious funerals as I accepted that having a service in a Church was inappropriate for some families. It seems dishonest to have a funeral in a Church for someone who had no affiliation, interest or emotional connection with a Church, to be buried from those facilities.

My instinct was saying this one needed a different approach. After putting together some form of service, I nervously asked about venue. To my surprise, they both asked could they have it in the Church. I was too scared to ask the reason. I did however ask about what I called the aftermath function. They asked about the options and I said one was that I could ask the Church ladies to do the catering, but we would expect a donation. They both quickly agree.

I returned to my office and sat down to reflect. The phone rang and it was Brent wanting to know how things unravelled. I took him through the arrangements and even he was surprised when he heard the venue was to be the Church.

"Do you have a cunning plan in mind?" he asked. I was not sure what I had in mind, but I knew I had a tough funeral ahead in a few days.

I rang one of our Churchwomen and asked would they do the catering, telling of the donation. I also explained this was a difficult funeral and could everyone just trust me - part of the reason for the request of trust was I had no idea what I was going to do.

Now I had a sermon to write as well as prepare a difficult funeral. This was going to need a lot of thought and I decided to park the sermon until after the funeral.

Brent arrived with the coffin about an hour before the service. He asked about my plan and I was still at a blank. I always helped him set up the coffin at the sanctuary end of our "hall"

Church and then went to put on my robes. The robes gave me a sense of psychological distance from what was about to happen.

The sister arrived first, walked in wearing a dark skirt suit, walked up the aisle and positioned herself on the left side of the Church. Her family was with her, but they hardly acknowledged that I existed. A few minutes later, the brother arrived with his wife and two young children. He walked down the aisle and sat on the right side of the Church. Even the friends took sides to show their support by sitting on the same side. We had an aisle that within my head I was calling "no man's land."

Brent wished me good luck when I started to walk up toward the front to start the service. As always, I stopped at the coffin, put both hands on it and stood in silence. I do this for two reasons: firstly, to break the taboo of the coffin; the second reason sounds stranger than the first - I want within myself to have a sense of connection with the deceased.

I went up to the lectern and started the service. No one was taking a bit of notice what I was saying and doing, they were glaring across the Church at each other; this was pathetic.

I then walked down and stood by the coffin. My notes left at the lectern. I talked about how we all deserve dignity when we die, no matter who we are. The deceased was a person who lived his life his way. He fathered two children and although he was a man of his generation, he never told his children he was proud of them, but beneath the exterior, I am confident he was proud.

It felt the closest to a sermon than anything I said on a Sunday and out of character for me. The tactic worked and they started to look towards the coffin. I didn't want them looking at me, but at the father they just lost.

At the end, I told the brother and sister to take either side of the coffin and get their respective families to help carry it out to the hearse. They reluctantly agreed. Once they lifted the coffin, they were instructed to look across at each other and remember the coffin was the force that actually joined them.

We got to the hearse without incident; I cannot describe the look on Brent's face as I couldn't interpret it.

I got them to say their farewell at the hearse and then took them to the hall for the aftermath food. Brother and sister held hands and walked together into the hall. I watched in disbelief. Brent touched my sleeve and said he knew I could fix the mess.

Afterwards the Churchwomen told me to go home and get a bottle of my wine. I needed to unwind over what had happened. I sneaked home and had a quick wee dram of whiskey. I needed something stronger than wine to unwind from this one.

40

Twenty-four hours of Church was a long time

It was not long after I started at the Parish that I set up a
worship committee. I was extremely aware that unless other
"voices" were involved I was going to make worship became
mechanical and boring.

During December/January I had the next year's lectionary in
place and would study all the readings for the coming year
and work out what was a theme. Running a Parish was no
different from running a good business, put the hard yards in
with high quality planning and the results can seem amazing.
Basic principles.

Working with the worship committee we did a huge amount
of statistical research on the make-up of the people within our
community not just the Church community, but our slice of
Palmerston North. We established there were basically five
different audiences, and so we set up five different forms of
worship to address each particular audience. The agreement
amongst us all was that we would keep this between
ourselves, for a while at least.

On paper it all sounded very easy, but in reality, it more than trebled my workload and meant the committee had to be very hands on. I was keen to do some post graduate study, to keep my mind active. I was determined to do a Master of Arts (History), but Suraya took me to a Massey University BBQ. There I met Frank, who was a lecturer in communication. Over a few too many glasses of red wine he talked me into doing a master's in business management, which duly happened.

One of the assignments for the communication course was to analyse the effectiveness of communication in an area we felt passionate about. For some strange reason I chose "the Church." I got my camera and drove around a number of Churches within Palmerston North. I took photos from the car when I got sight of the Church, up to the noticeboard. Then walked into each Church taking photos from the same sort of spot.

In the class, I opened by saying architecture speaks before we do. Then in silence showed the journey to each of the five Churches. I was the only one in the class with a religious disposition. The class was in hysterics at each Church. I showed my Church last and the others had no idea this was the Church I Ministered in. No change in reaction. My statement was the Church was supposed to be in the business of communication, but in reality, how well do they communicate?

I told the worship committee what I had done, and they wanted it made into a Church service, as a way of justifying what we were trying to do. I was nervous as to what reaction I would get. I used the slide show as a replacement for my sermon. One of the traditions I introduced was that after the sermon there was music for meditation – I had no input into the selection, so I was used to silence at this point. I could not read by the body language. At the end everyone left in silence. I was feeling sick to the core of my gut. I had not come to insult these beautiful people.

After each service there was a cup of tea in the hall at the back. I was traditionally the last one in, for a range of valid reasons. As I walked in, one of the men of the Parish approached me and I braced myself for the roasting. Instead he said he thought that was the most powerful sermon I had ever preached, and they all wanted to find out how to change. It was a unanimous agreement. This opened the door for those of us on the worship committee.

So, we had a rolling five-week style of worship. The fifth week was operating at a traditional level and was always the one we had the lowest attendance numbers. The one we had the largest numbers attending was the "Story Sunday." The worship committee was 100% running this service. It was based around a kids' story book and it always had a communion service aspect (which I led) using orange juice and round wine biscuits. Our Church could seat 180, but Story Sunday we were always overflowing, as word spread around the district. Our best was approximately close to 300 at one of those services. The Parish grew, but equally things were happening within me.

At one worship committee I said I was struggling with the fact that we had God locked in for an hour or two a week and we weren't engaging fully with our community. Over a number of meetings, it grew into us deciding we would hold a twenty-four-hour service. The Anglicans were two doors down from us and the Vicar and I got on extremely well. So, it was agreed we would hold twelve hours in each Church, with a ceremonial changing of Churches after twelve hours.

We decided to open the service with a shared Communion/Eucharist in our Church. Radio New Zealand was invited and recorded the two-hour opening. We had the Moderator of the Presbyterian Church and the Bishop of the Anglicans involved plus a range of lecturers and other clergy. During the night phase we had religious bands playing (all the neighbours were well informed – we never had a single complaint or niggle). Sleep was non-existent for 24 hours. We closed in St Matthews on the Sunday night, much the same way we started, except for two clergy who were the walking dead. It had a positive impact for both Churches as a lot of people from our district popped in to see "what was going on."

Our Church was buzzing and mad keen to do another. I didn't want to ever put my body through that experience again but had to admit a certain level of elation. We had certainly established ourselves as having a distinct point of difference. I have never forgotten it and never will.

41

Baby's technicolour

Shannon Parish was without a Minister and so I was their interim moderator. Translated into ordinary English this meant I was to play a fill-in Minister's role until we could get them a full-time Minister. The Parish was incredible and self-run to a huge extent, but I would go across to take communion services, baptisms and other special events. I had committed myself when at Knox that I was going to wear robes and so, even as a broke student, I bought a beautiful linen cassock which was technically white but had a sort of fawn fleck through it. I always wore it for services within the Church, but any weddings, funerals, etc., not directly with the Church, I just wore ordinary civilian street clothing.

The cassock was just a symbol; when I put it on, I felt I was in a servant role, and my personality ceased to exist. A young Shannon couple with no Church affiliation approached me to take their wedding. I happily agreed. What caught me off guard was they wanted to be married in the Church. We talked it through and agreed to have it in the Church.

Part of the reason they wanted me to take the service was that they already had a child and the word on the street was that I did not get upset about this. The only thing I encouraged them to do was have a vow in the service to their baby, symbolising this marriage wasn't just about them.

Suraya and I had done this as part of our wedding service; we wanted the kids to know our promise was to them as much as it was to each other. So, I shared what we had done with young couples, and each couple (with help and guidance from me) wrote a personalised vow to their child.

I have never taken the same wedding twice; same principle applied with funerals. Each service was unique as are the participants in each, and this service was to be no different.

I spent a lot of time with the young couple working through the dynamics of whom they are and why this thing called a wedding was important to them. I also wanted to establish what we would do to make sure their service was special, unique for them.

The day of the wedding arrived, and I met the groom when he arrived. The bride arrived a short time later with the little baby and her sister, who was to be bridesmaid and would hold the baby during the service until we got to the point of the vow to her.

The bride looked stunning and the service was going beautifully; being in the Church, I was in my cassock. The baby was very settled, and all boded well. The couple exchanged their vows in front of about twenty family and friends and now it was the baby's turn. I turned to the sister and nodded. This was the cue for me to hold the baby in front of her parents while they said their vows.

The sister passed the baby to me and I was going to bounce her for a few moments to make sure she was happy and gurgling. The little one had the strangest look on her face. I was still trying to work out why she has a funny colour in her face, when without warning she vomited a pink vomit all over the front of my robes. Then she started to gag, as though she was choking. I bent her across my arms and patted her back. Out came flying a huge lump of pink chewing gum onto the sanctuary floor with tears in hot pursuit. Thank goodness I was a parent. I stayed calm and cuddled the little one until she calmed down. Her beautiful (what had been white) gown was now as pink as mine. The Church was silent, frozen. One of the Parishioners who was there to help me disappeared out the back, returned with a wet tea towel and started to clean me up.

The congregation went from shock and horror to almost hysterical laughter. The bride was unsure whether to laugh or cry and the groom, well he stuck to tradition and was dumbstruck on the spot.

After a few moments I asked everyone to settle down and we continued with the Church lady cleaning me and the baby up. It was one wedding all those attending will never forget, with different levels of emotions and thoughts. Dry cleaners got my cassock back to new. I stayed in contact with the couple till I left the Parish.

A magical/special Christmas Eve

'Twas the season to be jolly. As a Parish Minister, this was true, but it was also your second busiest time of the year – Easter being the other.

We decided to have a number of services on Christmas Eve, as well as my taking two on Christmas Day. With us being a reconstituted family, our kids alternated Christmases with the other parent. This year Suraya and I were on our own.

I was obsessed about having themes for services, it kept me focussed. There was a 7:30p.m. service for young families, then a 9:30 for an older audience and the main service starting at 11:30p.m. on Christmas Eve. The Midnight service (as we called it) was being based around the carol "Silent Night." The idea was to finish the service with that carol and everyone walk out singing it.

I took it upon myself to get some genuine beeswax tapers for the midnight service. I wanted it to be a service none of us would forget, so I drove over to Whanganui one day to a supplier to the Catholic Church and bought a couple of boxes of the divinely smelling tapers. There was something about beeswax and how it impacts on the smell glands – love it.

The lead up to Christmas Eve was frantic, with all the services to prepare as well as all the other Christmas stuff families do. The weather forecast for Christmas Eve was not the greatest – fine but with strong winds. If any New Zealander takes the mickey out of Wellington for its wind, they have never lived in Palmerston North.

When I walked across to the Church for the 7:30 service, the wind was fair howling. I had a few thoughts that were more aligned to my Police Dog Handling days than those traditionally associated with a Minister. Translated, I hoped this lovely wind would die down and we could experience calm.

The 7:30 service was always the smallest; most kids were not going to be conned by their parents that this was a midnight service, and therefore had to go to bed straight away afterwards, otherwise Santa would not come. The service went without a hitch, the most memorable part was me wondering where the Church was going to end up when this wind finished its business with us. The wind certainly had the Church doing its own dance.

The 9:30 service was always slightly bigger, again with a slightly older congregation. I am sure the wind was teasing us, as it was getting more ferocious. The Church had originally been a hall and was put there as a temporary measure until the congregation could afford a "real Church." There was already a hall on the property when the "Church" arrived so a small administration block was put in to join the two buildings. They were functional, but architecturally dull.

The old building must have enjoyed its history of playing with the wind, as it was stubbornly refusing to be lifted off its piles.

Then the service that was to be the *piece d'resistence*. The hard part on the breaks between services like this was wanting to take a Nano nap, risking forgetting to wake up in time for the next, so I never took that risk.

I got over to the Church at about 11 and opened it up, dressed in my cassock, and lit the "Christ Candle" on the Communion table in the middle of the sanctuary at the front. I arrived in Palmerston North just before Christmas. One day I was walking the local shops and a florist had this massive white candle in the middle of her display. I went in and asked about buying it. She would not sell it to me before Christmas as her floral display in the window was drawing in many customers, but straight after Christmas I was able to go in and buy it from her.

The candle was about two feet tall with a very thick girth.

Not long after I arrived the members of our Choir began to assemble. and they started to sing carols as others were arriving. Everyone, including Choir, was given a beeswax taper and advised this would be used at the end of the service.

In case you are wondering, yes, the wind had not eased off, if anything it became slightly faster. These services were wonderful, because you get to meet the extended families, plus the ones who only came at Christmas and Easter. Personally, it never bothered me that some only came twice a year – it was not for me to judge them at any level, and we always welcomed everyone.

One thing Christmas does, with the singing of the traditional carols, the singing goes up a number of notches. The Choir allowed us to introduce new carols, as they were brilliant at leading the singing. Wendy, our musical director, was a superstar as far as I was concerned.

We were getting near the end of the service and close to singing "Silent Night." We were going back to the original tradition and having no accompaniment. I had briefed a couple of our youth group members and on my signal came to the "Christ Candle" and lit theirs. I also lit my own.

The lights were turned off and then these young people walked down the aisle lighting the tapers at the aisle. Standing at the front, it was almost like a Disney script as the flickering candle light spread through the whole Church. The Church was battened down because of the wind, and so the lovely beeswax scent drifted through the whole building.

We sang the first verse of "Silent Night," and then at the end of that one I walked down the aisle with mine, listening to the wind howling almost as much as the singing. A couple of our Parish people opened the doors so I could walk out. As they opened the doors, the wind stopped, and I mean stopped. There was not a whisper of wind.

Suraya came out with her taper and stood by me and slowly the congregation came out, still singing. No one spoke, we all just nodded to each other and watched these tapers flicker and dance down the streets of Awapuni until they went into their homes.

Suraya went home to put the kettle on while I went back into the Church, locked it up and got out of my cassock. The smells of beeswax still massaging my senses.

We had our cup of tea, hardly speaking for what we had been through – what a memorable Christmas Eve, never to be forgotten.

43

An unexpected visit from the Police

One of my Parishioners, Shirley, quickly identified I wasn't a traditional Parish Minister. After Church one Sunday she pulled me to one side and said she was involved with a community group that was setting up a local Victims Support Group. She invited me to join with them. I was so new and wanting to get the Parish up and going I delayed attending so it wouldn't look like I had rushed into non-Parish work.

Shirley left it a number of months and then approached me again. She explained the workload would not be excessive because the Police were now involved and had dedicated a Detective Senior Sergeant (John) to take a very active role. Shirley had decided John and I would get on extremely well. So, I decided perhaps now was the time to do it.

I went to my first meeting and after polite introductions, basically sat and listened. John came up after the meeting and said he heard I used to be in the job. I explained that I had been a Dog Handler at Hamilton and left for the Church. I could see John trying to process a Dog Handler and Church in the same sentence.

The following meeting went along, and John was explaining to everyone that we needed a formal launch, which meant a more formal committee to run the show. He said he did not want to be the inaugural chair, as it looked too much like a Police event rather than a community event. Everyone nodded in agreement. I put my hands under my bum to stop me volunteering. John then announced to the group that he thought I should be the Chair as I was the only genuine victim of a serious crime amongst the group. Everyone turned and looked at me. I was flummoxed. This came completely from left field and I did not have an instant retort in my head.

Before I could gather my thoughts, John asked me to tell the group my story. He had obviously been making some phone calls, because I hadn't told him what I had been through. I started to shake, as talking out loud to a group of strangers about that night was a few steps too far as far as I was concerned. I said a few silent words to the boss and took some deep breaths. The scene had been set and I had no escape. All these expectant faces staring at me waiting for the birth of my story.

I started slowly, my voice shuddering, my eyes starting to swell, my heart racing. The only way I could get through this was to pretend no one else was present and be back giving evidence at the trial. The tactic worked well until I got to the actual stabbing; uncontrollable tears flooded over my cheeks, but I kept talking. I stopped the story when I was put in the Ambulance.

John looked at me and told me it was the best acceptance speech he had ever heard. All the others came up and hugged me, led of course by Shirley. This was the first she knew of this happening to me. I just wanted to get in the car and get out of the place.

I had been outvoted and became Chair of Manawatu Victims Support Group. We settled in at the next meeting developing a work plan. The first thing was to create awareness. John (like he always did) got his way. He was organising a number of public events the Police would market and I was to be the key note speaker at each one. I had another interesting conversation with John as to what I thought of this. As usual John won, and I did numerous public events.

John and I became very close through this process and caught up most weeks. He was a very impressive boss, so I was surprised one day when he rang and asked could he come and see me. His voice had that official Policeman tone. This made me ask in what capacity was he coming and he gave his rank, etc., saying it was an official visit. I was puzzled as to why I was getting a formal visit from the Police.

I knew it would not take long for him to get from the Police Station, so I went ahead and made us both a cup of coffee. John duly arrived and he had a worried look on his face.

When I offered him a coffee, he told me he thought it was inappropriate for the reason why he was here. This certainly got my interest, but also raised warning bells as to what was actually going on.

John wanted to know why I was going to Ashhurst so frequently and I explained I was interim moderator for the Parish, same as I was for Shannon. He kept asking me what I thought were strange questions, and I was starting to get annoyed, so I demanded to know what the hell was all of this about.

He asked if I knew a particular street and a particular house. I told him of course I did, and I got this real weird look of horror from him. He then asked why, and I said I was taking a home wedding for the lady of the house, who was the bride.

John instantly relaxed, which added to the mystery for me. He made a few more probing questions and I was able to show him documentation to prove what I was saying was true.

Now I wanted answers, why was I being treated like a criminal. I knew one of his portfolios was vice, so he then told me his team was doing a stake out on the house and there were two Ministers going to this same address, and I was obviously one. The house was a local brothel and my bride was the "Madam." John was very professional and never gave clues as to who the other Minister was, but we ended up in raucous laughter, once we got the serious stuff behind us.

NB: The Police held off with their raid until after the wedding, which they had checked out was legitimate. The bride never knew what I went through, but it was a giggle.

44

Tough Love

John knew about my "Parents of Teenagers" group, so one day he asked me had I ever heard of the "Tough Love" programme. I had not, so he explained what it was about and would I be prepared to set one up for Palmerston North. I was sure I could manage on less sleep, so said yes.

John had another parent who he wanted to join with me to be co-leaders for the local programme. He arranged for us both to meet at the Police Station, as the Police were going to be the sponsors as well as providers of families in need. Tom was not what I expected. He was English, professional working at the University, dressed in his suit and a really neat guy. We got on like a house on fire.

We both agreed to jointly lead the programme and John set up for our first night and he would provide the audience. He sent us both home with a ton of reading material so we could actually understand what we were supposed to do.

The literature was very strong on saying "tough love" was not for the kids, it was tough on the parents, and we were to learn the truth of that philosophy.

John set up rooms for our meetings, away from the Police Station, out of respect for the parents. Our first session we had about eight sets of parents turn up. We opened up with Tom and I explaining why we had set this up. Tom left me speechless; he told the story of how their son was a monster. They had two wonderful daughters who caused them no problems and then their son was the complete opposite. I struggled with the notion Tom would have problems at home, knowing what types of stories we were about to hear.

After we'd done our bit, we asked each set of parents to tell their story. What I was not prepared for was the similarity to Tom's story; they all had one child they could not control, while all the others were terrific kids. The literature said this would be the case, but my Police experience was about "bad families." The concept was that to change the kid's behaviour, you had to change your own. As parents we got into patterns/rituals that the kids knew, but equally knew how to use those patterns/rituals to fire their parents up.

I will share one story without identifying the parties involved. One mother explained that her teenage twin girls would fight all the time, even tearing hair out of each other. She was the only one who had more than one misbehaving, but the story was powerful as to how tough love works. We got the mother to describe to us all the dynamics that ended in these two girls fighting. It was difficult to digest, as all these parents in the room were incredibly special, middleclass, hardworking, caring, neat people.

After listening to her, we told her she needed to go away and think through how she responded and then when the next situation arose, do the opposite of what the girls expected.

The following week, the mother walked into our session with a smile that was bigger than her whole face. She physically looked rejuvenated, alive and excited. Everyone agreed we wanted to hear her story first.

She described how she'd gone to the small kitchen to prepare the evening meal. Her daughters were in the lounge which was off the kitchen. She got the potatoes out, putting them into the sink, washing them to start the peeling process. The girls were starting to niggle each other. The mother's stomach tensed up, tying a Gordian knot inside of her. She was about to scream at them to stop when she remembered our advice – do the opposite of what you would normally do. The knowledge of what she planned calmed her down, even though the swearing and fisticuffs between the girls was gaining momentum.

Gently and quietly, she put the potato peeler in the sink, walked slowly outside to the back wall of the house. Attached to the wall was the garden hose. She uncoiled it, turned the tap on full and slowly walked back into the house, carrying the hose. Through the kitchen she strolled and into the lounge, water spraying everywhere. She just aimed it at the girls and blasted them with the hose, saying nothing. The stunned girls looked in disbelief at their mother. The mother never spoke and when she decided they had learnt their lesson, she returned the journey for the hose, taking time to put it away properly. She then walked into the kitchen, never said a word, picked up the potato peeler and carried on as usual.

The daughters were in stunned mullet mode, just standing staring at the kitchen. When Mum carried on preparing the meal, as though nothing had happened, the two daughters took it upon themselves to clean everything up.

When the Mum finished telling the group, we had our own clean up to do. Everyone, once they recovered from the shock of what they had heard, went into hysterical laughter. I caught up with that mother two years later, down the street, with her angelic daughters. She just winked and smiled when she saw me.

Tom and I became great friends, and when I was at Massey I would frequently pop in and say hi to him in his office. Then one Sunday afternoon, my phone rang. It was Tom in an almost hysterical voice. Could I get around to his house asap as their son was out of control. I rushed there with no idea what to expect. It was winter and I could see the smoke coming out of their chimney.Walking briskly up their driveway I heard elevated voices, one being Tom's. I called out and Tom yelled for me to come in the lounge as fast as I could. He sounded unbelievably over the stress barrier.

I rushed into the lounge and there was Tom's son, holding his mother above his head, trying to throw her into the open fire, with Tom physically trying to prevent this from happening. I bellowed at the son to put his mother down or I would put him down. The tactic worked, the poor mother was uncontrollably crying, understandably so.

I spent some time with the son, explaining my past and what the consequences of his actions would mean for him if he ever did it again. He'd heard this speech many a time, but calmed down enough for me to safely leave a few hours later. I didn't know how the family coped, I'd met the daughters who were as wonderful as Tom had described. A very normal, great family, with one child who was out of control. Society will be quick to blame the parents, but you wouldn't find people who worked so hard at being great parents. I would never understand what caused this or how it all happened.

45

A funeral that changed my style

My mate, Paul, the Minister of St David's was taking annual leave, an-easier-said-than-done exercise for a Parish Minister. He asked if I could just do funeral coverage for him, as he had everything else organised. No problem.

I was working in my office on the next Sunday's service when the phone rang. It was Robert the funeral director. He explained that he had a death of the spouse of one of the members of St David's and was I covering for Paul, which got an affirmative response. I wrote down the details, went and changed into a clerical collar, and drove to the given address.

As usual with these things, when you arrived there was already a gathering of cars as friends and family arrive to share what had happened.

I went in and introduced myself to the new widow, then met everyone. It was a stinking hot day and I was offered a cup of tea or coffee. I declined and asked for a cold drink, thinking nothing of it. A few minutes later the deceased's adult son handed me a beautiful, icy cold beer. I could not believe my luck. I thanked him and took a swig and went back to the conversation. I realised I was looking at a bunch of stunned mullets, eyes bulging, jaw dropped syndrome.

The son said, "you actually drink beer?" which I affirmed. The room quickly emptied and, in a few minutes, they were all back with their "cold ones." We had a hilarious time as we talked about the husband/father who had dropped dead from a massive heart attack. I was there about two hours, as it takes that long to sense who the deceased was as a person.

Then the son who'd given me the drink challenged me. "You didn't know my Dad and there's no way you can take a funeral that reflects him." I loved a challenge, so I challenged him back to tell me after the service whether I had done his Dad's life true justice.

When I got in the car, I admonished myself for making such a challenge with no idea of how I was going to make this happen.

In the lead up to the service I saw the family a minimum of once a day. I went to the funeral directors and asked to see the body. I wanted to say hi to the guy for whose funeral I was responsible.

The day of the funeral arrived, and I was there greeting everyone, dressed in my cassock, etc. Murray, the deceased, was a foreman on a construction gang, and a larger than life character. Here was a religious bozo going to take his funeral. For many attending, their tone of voice, body language and other nuances, while polite, were obviously sceptical.

As I have always done at a funeral, I walked up to the front, stood at the coffin, put my hands on it and said a silent prayer.

Many people are scared of death and coffins and my gesture showed there was nothing to fear. From my perspective, I showed respect for the deceased as a real person.

We did the opening part of the service, which the family had requested, then it was my time to take the eulogy. I explained I had never met Murray while he was alive, but through symbols I could let them have their own memories of him. I picked up one of the props I had in the sanctuary, a full bag of cement. I did not hold it for long as those things are darned heavy. I talked about how Murray would walk around the construction sites with one under each arm. I asked them in silence to remember that image of him. I then did the same with a pool cue, Murray's poker pack of cards, a Gin bottle, and then some photos of family time. After each item, there was silent, reflective time. After using each item, it was laid on the ground, near the coffin but far enough away for the pall bearers to do their upcoming task.

The time came to carry the coffin out of the Church; all the pall bearers were burly construction workers, all with tears running down their cheeks as they paid tribute to their mate. They carried him out unashamedly weeping the whole distance. Once at the hearse I stood to one side, as they didn't need a Holy Roller anymore, all being there for one another. We had said the words of committal in the Church, so it was all over now.

I was going back into the Church to take off my cassock and get into cooler clothing. I just about jumped out of my skin when tapped on my shoulder. It was the son who had challenged me. He had an envelope and a bottle of whiskey. He wanted me to take them and I said the funeral director looks after me in that regard (sadly never the whiskey part).

The widow told the son I would win the challenge, so he came to the service prepared to pay "his dues." He was crying as he told me his dad could not have had a better send off.

It was strange for others to comprehend, but I liked taking funerals, because I felt practical. My funerals going forward from Murray's involved a lot of symbols about the deceased as they spoke louder to the family than any flowery words I could ever dream.

46

Bible in school went down an unexpected path

I was approached to do Bible in school at a local primary, and not being able to think of a reason to say no, I did it. My educational passion was adult learners, as I didn't see myself as being very good with the younger audience, but no one said being a Minister was easy.

I think the Principal (Jane) watched me struggling with it all, so she asked me when I was leaving one day, would I object to being shifted to a different class. I wasn't sure how to take the query, until she explained they had a class of young people who were, to put it politely, wayward. So, I agreed.

One day Jane decided to visit the class unexpectedly while I was taking a session. When she walked in, I had one boy in my left hand, swinging above the ground, and another in my right, with me carrying on as though this was normal. The other kids were paying 100% attention to everything I said, were well behaved, never called out, but rather politely raised their hand to ask questions. Jane said nothing, watched for a while and then left. I expected to get the bullet.

A couple of weeks later Jane rang me and asked would I mind coming to her office later that day – firing squad was the phrase going through my mind.

I duly arrived at Jane's office, bringing back school day memories of going to the Principal office to get a lovely piece of bamboo cane across my behind. It took a long time to realise that Principal's offices are used for things beyond removing the dust from our trousers.

I confess to having sweaty hands as I sat in the chair opposite her.

Jane was a young, ambitious, intelligent and clever woman. She jumped the promotion queue by taking on a problem school for which no one else was game enough. She explained how she was working with the kids on a daily basis to improve their attitude towards life and education.   The problem was they went back to the same seriously dysfunctional homes at the end of the day, all the good work of the school undone. In my head I was trying to work out how this conversation was heading towards a bullet between my eyes. I knew what she was saying was true, because of the delightful little fellows I had for Bible in School.   I think they had a roster amongst themselves as to who would misbehave the most so they would be held in the air.

Jane explained she needed to do something to change the home situation, something a school does not have a mandate to do. Most of the students I "looked after" were looking at expulsion because their behaviour was having a significant negative impact on other students.   Jane's suggested approach, was for me to run a parenting group to train the parents how to "do their job." It all sounds easy when you say it quickly, but the practical reality was difficult. Loving an impossible challenge, I accepted.

I had three weeks to prepare and Jane gave me the staff room to run the group, who she saw as her responsibility to get them there. My walk back to home had my mind doing gymnastics at what I was taking on.

I prayed, read, thought, meditated, prayed some more for divine inspiration. A week out from the start and I still had no idea what I was going to do.

One of the Parish ladies popped in and saw me, telling me about her "difficult" teenage son. We talked it through and after she left, I realised I was relying on my Uni Paper "Human Growth and Development." So, I dived into my old textbooks, converting the material into street language and world view. My problem was solved.

At the end of the first session, I was more than blown away at the positive response I got from all these mums. The second session, they were all early, like pieces of blotting paper sniffing out ink to absorb. Jane was seeing a change in the kids, behaviour at school, except for one delightful character – if anything he was worse. She wanted me to focus on this mum at the next session.

I thought, prayed and came up with an approach, knowing I would be flying by the seat of my pants. When the mums all arrived, I went around them one at a time asking how they thought these sessions were helping them, leaving the aforementioned mum till last.

The group was learning so much about their children, but equally a huge amount about themselves. I got to the last mum. She said she was getting very little out of the sessions because her son wasn't changing. So, I asked her to describe the household dynamics when her son got home from school.

"When Johnny (*not true name*) gets home from school I'm watching my soaps. He keeps interrupting and asking stupid questions." She paused, so I asked her to tell us what happened next.

"Well he was such a bloody nuisance, and he knows how to wind me up that I belt him one."

How strong was the belt?

"He flies across the room and hits the wall. He knows he has gone too far when he pushes me to that point, so he goes and sulks in his room."

The answer as to what to do next was obvious to me. I explained to the group that "mum" and I are going to do a role play, and I want none of them to say anything until I ask them for feedback. The "mum" had a quizzical look on her face.

We set the room up as Johnny's lounge at home. I explained to mum she was to be Johnny and I will play her. Johnny was to come home from school, excited because the teacher told him how clever he was today. So, I sent the mother out of the room, I lounged in a chair watching the TV. (There was an actual TV in the room.) Action. She opens the door and came in really excited, wanting to tell me how great her day was. I just start abusing her, telling her to shut up as I am watching my favourite soap. She carries on so I get up and go to her to give her a hiding. She breaks down crying. I stopped the role play at this point. No one was allowed near the mum.

We put the room back to how we had it before, and then I asked the mum, "Why are you crying?"

"Because you scared me." I then turned to the group for their input. They worked with the mum to explain that what she did to Johnny when he got home from school was identical to what I did to her.

We completely debriefed before finishing, and every couple of days I visited the mum at her home to make sure she was ok. Our rule was what happened in the group stayed in the group.

About two weeks later, Jane approached me after one of our sessions. She asked what had happened at "that session." I explained that group confidentiality was the reason I couldn't tell her. She smiled at me and said that was a huge turning point for Johnny and his mum. They had a totally different boy at school now, but so had all the kids of the mums who attended our group. Jane could not believe, how her school had changed in such a short space of time. I didn' tell her I was the most amazed. [1]

---

[1] Don't try this. I was trained in Psycho-drama and counselling and have never used this approach a second time.

47

Drink driving was naughty

The Anglican Church and ours were separated by one house, owned by a delightful elderly couple. I was never sure how they felt, but they had the two Ministers visit them. Frank was Presbyterian and Joyce, his wife, was Anglican. They alternated weeks at each other's Churches and were very popular with both congregations.

Life has its unique way of sorting us out, and Frank was deteriorating through old age. It was not a pleasant process to watch or experience, especially if you have all your faculties, which Frank did. Eventually he was admitted to Hospital, where he was to die. In those times, hospices did not exist, and the system really did not know how to care for the elderly.

In his day, Frank would have been a debonair, dashing tall guy, with a full mop of hair. His wife Joyce, obviously an eye turner in her day. Now they were an elderly couple with all the prerequisite thinning grey hairs, and wrinkles where once had been smooth skin.

They were deeply affectionate towards each other, gazing into the other's eyes as teenagers in full lust mode. I enjoyed both of them and shared many magnificent cups of tea with them.

When Frank was admitted to Palmerston North Hospital, I promised Joyce I would visit every day, a promise I kept. How does one describe what it feels like, to watch the life slowly ebb out of a beautiful person? Joyce was there every day and the family had come to "look after Mum and wait for the inevitable for Dad." It was toughest on Joyce, in love since teenage years with the same man and watching him gradually slip away.

Joyce made one request of me: would I make sure I was present when Frank died, and of course I said yes.

It was an excruciatingly slow process, and I had no idea which day was going to be his last, so as time went on, I was staying for longer and longer visits. I still had to do all the other duties a Minister does, and one certainly doesn't become a Minister for the pay or believe in a 40-hour week. One does it for times like journeying through a faithful servant's death, to be there, experience the draining stress, to provide comfort to the numb, and always, always see it as a privilege that you are journeying with this family.

Through the regular visits I got to know the staff on his ward, especially the Doctors, who saw me as an integral part of the "care" team. One evening the Doctor walked in to do the usual check up on Frank. When he finished, he just stood and watched Frank, then turned and told us all he thought Frank would go tonight. He then looked me in the eye, telling me I had to go home and get some rest, as my real work was about to begin and I would need every reserve of energy to be able to continue to support the family.

Joyce took my hand and promised me they would ring when it was nearly the end, so I would have time to get back. I was happy to stay the night, but I also knew the Doctor and Joyce were right about me, but also, I sometimes felt like an intruder in this family's sacred time.

I went home, and as usual Suraya asked how Frank was going. I told her and we just sat silently for a short time. Then I decided I needed a whiskey to relax me so I could get some sleep. I decided to go straight to bed, even though it was early evening. Trained as an on-call Dog Handler, I set up my "Minister" clothes at the end of the bed, and yes, my trusty gumboots. I was asleep less than an hour when the call came for me to get back to the Hospital as quickly as possible. It took next to no time to be dressed and in the car.

I realised I still had whiskey on my breath but did not stress. I was unsure whether I was over the limit, because it was a small drink, but I also knew tiredness plays a part in how alcohol impacts on you. I eventually turned left into Ruahine Street, only minutes from the Hospital. Ahead were flashing Police lights. As I approached, I realised it was a Police Drink/Drive bus, stopping all cars. Internally, I started to sweat.

I lowered my driver's window and slowed down. An Officer approached me and asked if I had been drinking. I had my clerical collar on, explaining I was rushing to the Hospital for a dying Parishioner and did not have time for this. He apologised and waved me through. Now I was shaking as much externally as internally.

I looked in my rear mirror and saw a Police car pull out and start to follow me. I turned left into the Hospital car park and roared through the reasonably empty car park to park as close to the ward as possible. The pesky cop was still following me. I parked, jumped out of the car and ran across towards the ward, gumboots and all. Into the ward and as quick plus quiet as possible I flew down the corridor.

I went into Frank's room and he was already dead. My heart sank and I looked for Joyce. The family told me she had to go to the toilet and that was when Frank decided enough was enough. I could hear the door start to open, and it was Joyce returning; standing on the other side was the cop. He realised we had a death in there, just nodded to me and wandered away.

Joyce, later on, was able to laugh about it all, that Frank made sure he went in a private manner and that maybe the boss was involved somehow in letting him have his way, this final time.

Frank's funeral was special (as they all are), but as a Minister it was impossible not to get close to the people; so, you carry their pain as well as acknowledging your own. It was a tough funeral, but they were often the ones I felt best about.

48

My inner voice was misbehaving again

Suraya was a producer at the Massey University Television Production Unit. Massey was the largest University in New Zealand for distance education students. She was an extremely talented producer and I always took pride in her work. My gorgeous wife made incredible productions. She also had an amazing team, and one guy had the most wicked sense of humour.

I was doing my post graduate studies on campus, so I was up there as much as time allowed and frequently popped in to see her.

This particular day, I had my clerical collar on for some reason. All her crew knew I was a Minister but had never seen me with the dog collar on. Suraya's crew was putting up a set that was to be a student flat. On one of her inspections she told them the flat looked too clean and normal, that this was supposed to look like a true student's flat.

As I walked in, one of the real characters had just finished spray painting graffiti on the wall, and he stepped back to admire his handiwork. He got a shock when he heard me burst out laughing from behind – he was unaware I was present. The set crew went rigid.

The graffiti read, "Easter is cancelled this year, they found the body." Eventually the others woke up to the fact I was laughing, and I did not find the posting offensive. When they grilled my why, it was very simple. My faith was not based on something like a dead body, and if they found the body of Jesus it would have zero impact on me.

We all chuckled and later I left. But my mind did not leave. No, the graffiti was not offensive to me, but people expect certain things from a Minister. I was internally wrestling with the ethics of feeling I had to say what the Church publicly said, rather than address the issues I was concerned about.

Over the next months I talked with a few confidents, and I mean a few. I only spoke with one fellow clergyman, because he was the only one, I knew I could honestly tell what was happening within me and would not judge me. I felt as though I had a calling to leave being a Parish Minister and do something totally non-traditional.

The decision to look elsewhere and leave the Parish was gut wrenching. I applied for a lecturing role in Auckland and was accepted. I had to ring my Session Clerk and tell her the news as well as my Minister Mentor. The Parish organised an amazing farewell. I was stunned at how many people appeared genuinely upset that I was leaving. A Church that was on the brink of closing when I arrived, was now alive, vibrant, and yet within me I never felt successful.

Ministers work horrendous hours, deal with a myriad of situations you cannot talk to anyone else about. You are meant to epitomise family life, and yet to do the Parish work, your family plays second fiddle. I did not resign my ordination; it was always sacred to me as it was all those years ago. I just resigned from my Parish. I hope the few stories I have shared show I loved what I did.

Postscript

A lot of water has gone under the bridge since I left Parish Ministry. I worked in the corporate world, not for profit and vocational training in what I believe was an unofficial form of Chaplaincy. My career was very successful (from my perspective).

In 2016 we sold up in Auckland, moving to Rotorua to set up our own not for profit to help Māori Youth into apprenticeships, then in July 2017 my past tsunamied back into my life.

The delightful young fellow who ran a knife through me, rearranging my body, mind and soul, fatally shot two women who walked onto the property he was renting in Northland. The first I knew of this was the media ringing me and I was suddenly, unexpectedly a person of significant interest to them.

I was falling apart and so I talked to my GP about it. She suggested counselling, but I turned it down, believing I would be alright as I adjusted to the news, Patterson had taken his own life. My secret fear of him coming back to get me should be all over.

Our trust financially fell over, so we sold up and shifted to Waiuku to semi-retire. A number of friends told me they believed I was suffering PTSD (Post Traumatic Stress Disorder), which I foolishly rejected. Suraya sat me down and explained what I was like to live with and that I needed to get help. It was incredibly tough to try and dispassionately look at myself and realise maybe I was not in good shape. The thought of going to another Doctor and bursting into tears did not appeal. I needed to work through everything, so I wrote a letter to my GP, set up an appointment, presented him with the letter, saying no talking was allowed until he read it.

Eventually he said he would be back shortly, and he left the surgery. When he came back, he said he was going to try and get me treated for PTSD under the ACC system. He was going to manage the paperwork and for me not to worry. We talked about my medications, but I did not want them to change. Years before I'd had heart by-pass surgery that the Cardiac Surgeon told me he believed was an outcome of the stress of the Police career.

I had also had major back surgery, again attributable to my time in the Police.

Eventually I was accepted by ACC and assigned a case manager. He recommended a Psychologist that they would fund my treatment.

A short time later I had my first session. I cried uncontrollably through the session and I remember saying "when will this ever end?" Over a number of months, I came to realise the reality was that I suffered PTSD for over 30 years, burdening my wife and family. The treatment journey was lumpy and bumpy, but gradually the sun started to break through the clouds.

I cannot change the past, and in a strange way I am grateful for it, as it has shaped me into the person I now am. In saying that, in one session I described myself being a dog on a very tight choke chain, reacting and responding through fear. Through high quality, sensible therapy, the choke chain has gone and I now I know a level of freedom within myself, that I never could have comprehended in the past.

In February 2020, I left a meeting in the Waiuku township and was walking back to my car. It was about 7pm, a lovely starlight night, still muggy with the drought we were experiencing. I walked past a premise and in the driveway was an altercation. One young lady was trying to remove the head of a young guy with a baseball bat. I felt all my "old triggers" start to kick into gear. The heart racing, chest tightening, adrenaline pumping and as quick as I felt it, I managed to stop it, using techniques I had been taught during therapy. The nature of the incident warranted the Police being called, so I quickly and quietly retreated into a shop doorway and rang the Police emergency.

During the call I listened to my voice, I was calm rational, objective as I relayed what was happening. After the Police arrived and took control, I gave one of the officers my business card, explaining I was the one who called. I then walked to my car and drove home.

I feel compelled to say here that this was the first "incident" I had seen since living in Waiuku. It was the friendliest community I have every lived in, so please treat this incident as an isolated one.

A few days later I told my wife what had happened. I had gone home, eaten dinner and later went to bed, having a very relaxed sleep.

At one of my therapy sessions I was asked how I thought it was going and I wrote the following list:

- I now stop and constructively self-analyse what I am doing or thinking as opposed to the past of destructive self-analyst
- I am constantly evaluating my own thoughts and actions
- I regularly practice "Mindfulness" exercises
- I am always looking for the positive, rather than the negative
- I have far better-quality sleep than I can ever remember
- I reflect, and positively change the way I talk to my wife and family. This has been the hardest part to come to terms with, how destructive I have been to those I love
- I focus on kindness as opposed to "being nice"
- I am now very mindful of my physiological reactions, which are the initial warning triggers of old ways of thinking and behaviours. I use exercise to calm myself down
- I not only enjoy life, I love it
- I don't have to prove myself so much, especially to myself. I have always been extremely tough on myself
- I view life through a healthier lens
- As with the story in Waiuku I record factual, actual concrete evidence of when I successfully manage myself through a trigger response. This was to rewire my brain, so that I can actually like me for the first time in more years than I can remember.

Diagnosed with Prostate Cancer, not long after moving to Waiuku and this year with type 2 diabetes. I know darkness, but now I far prefer light and intend to annoy others by staying alive for many years to come. Our lives are not straight-line graphs, some have more bumps than others, those are what create character within our personality.

Journeying through life, many people touch, move, challenge, make us grow. Changing style of Dog Collar was right for me and I still wear one of those over thirty years later.

Humans operate best in some form of community, isolating yourself does not work. The sad thing for me was everyone I have ever met has an interesting story to tell, and I wish they would take the time, even if it was just for the sake of family, to record their life stories or, as I have done, part of them.

All our stories are unique, and so is yours.

I hope and pray you have enjoyed this collection, and maybe with a bit of luck someone else might have gotten fresh insight into life, themselves, their work or the Church.

Life is for living, thank you for reading, enjoy your life, for it is a precious gift.

www.ingramcontent.com/pod-product-compliance
Lightning Source LLC
Chambersburg PA
CBHW060230050426
42448CB00009B/1377